D1459296

RAILWAY WALKS

GWR & SR

For Denis Baxter
without whose enthusiasm and vision
this project might never have been started

RAILWAY WALKS

GWR & SR

JEFF VINTER

ALAN SUTTON

First published in the United Kingdom in 1990 by
Alan Sutton Publishing Limited · Brunswick Road · Gloucester

First published in the United States of America in 1990 by
Alan Sutton Publishing Inc · Wolfeboro Falls · NH 03896–0848

British Library Cataloguing in Publication Data

Vinter, Jeff
Railway walks: GWR & SR
1. Southern England – Visitors' guides
I. Title
914.22′04858

ISBN 0-86299-578-7
ISBN 0-86299-722-4 pbk

Library of Congress Cataloging in Publication Data applied for

Cover illustrations: Left: Crossing keeper's cottage at Cater's Cottage near
Brockenhurst, looking towards Ringwood. *Right:* A short (and very shallow)
bridge-cum-tunnel between Serridge Junction and Drybrook Road in the
Forest of Dean.

Typeset in 10/12 Plantin.
Typesetting and origination by
Alan Sutton Publishing Limited.
Printed in Great Britain by
Dotesios Printers Limited.

CONTENTS

ACKNOWLEDGEMENTS

In any book of this sort, a large number of individuals and organizations are bound to have lent a helping hand. Particular thanks are due to the following:

For accommodation and sustenance: Guy and Sue Sheppard, Exeter; Adam and Eddie McGregor, Padstow; and John and Doreen Hodge, Stonehouse. My wife and I were on the road for many weeks in the preparation of this book and greatly appreciated a homely welcome.

For access to books: Alan Vinter, my father; Pete Walker, fellow railway rambler; and Robert Turner and the staff of Winchester Library. Without the library's excellent Railway Collection, the histories in this book could not have been nearly so thorough. Thanks are also due to the staff of Stroud Library, who provided enough local information to piece together a history of the largely undocumented Nailsworth branch.

For their personal reminiscences: Reg Ridd, Padstow; James Winstanley, Chichester; William Malpas, Nailsworth; John and Joyce Dickers, South-bourne; David Franks, Whitwell; and Mike Rees, Coleford.

For proof-reading and corrections: my wife, Jenny; the late Brian Lyndon; Neil Mitchell, Countryside Ranger with West Sussex County Council; and John Hill of the Cranleigh and District Conservation Volunteers.

For information on railway walks: Rhys ab Elis, whose *Railway Rights of Way* was a veritable bible throughout this project; the staff of Sustrans Ltd, Bristol; the staff of the Forestry Commission, Coleford; and Mr M.J. Fleming of Wealden District Council. Paul Richardson of British Rail also provided valuable information on recent and future railway developments on the Isle of Wight.

For information on rural bus services: the Ramblers Association, for making generally available Jennifer Howard's invaluable list of council bus information offices. This was published initially in *ATCO News*, the journal of the Association of Transport Co-ordinating Officers.

For numerous soakings: the British climate and my own unerring ability to choose all the wet days simply by looking at a calendar.

For transport and rescue services: my wife, Jenny, who was always there at the end of the walk, no matter how late the hour or remote the location. Without her willingness to accept the demands imposed on us both by this project, this book could never have been written.

JV

LOCATION OF WALKS

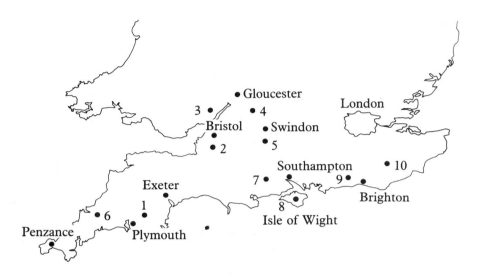

1. The Plym Valley Railway Path and Cycle Route
2. The Cheddar Valley Railway Walk
3. The Forest of Dean
4. The Stroud Valleys Pedestrian Cycle Trail
5. The Midland and South Western Junction Railway, Wiltshire
6. The Camel Trail
7. The New Forest
8. The Isle of Wight
9. The Downs Link
10. The Cuckoo Trail

KEY TO MAPS

Railways

——————————— Railway path

- - - - - - - - - - - Course of trackbed (no public access)

▬▬▬▬▬▬▬▬▬ Operational railway

Stations

————■———— With buildings and platforms

————●———— With platforms only

————○———— Station site (few remains if any)

Features

══════════ Viaduct or major bridge

—)————(— Tunnel with through access

—)- - - - -(— Tunnel with no through access

SH Goods or engine shed

SB Signal-box

LC Level crossing with keeper's cottage, crossing gates or rails *in situ*

Other Routes

═══════════ Any metalled road

······················· Track or path

Facilities

⊂▷ Public house nearby

Note: The relevant Ordnance Survey maps are identified in the 'Transport and Facilities' section of each chapter.

INTRODUCTION

The fourth chapter of John Betjeman's autobiography in verse, *Summoned by Bells*, begins with a delightful evocation of a train journey along the Southern Railway's former North Cornwall line from Launceston to Wadebridge. Betjeman alighted at Wadebridge, but the line continued for another six glorious miles along the Camel estuary to the fishing town of Padstow, its narrow streets piled up on the steep hillside that leads down to the harbour. Trains ceased to run from Launceston to Wadebridge on 3 October 1966, but the Padstow section survived until 30 January 1967, thanks to a separate line which ran to Bodmin.

When the trains had gone, the line entered a curious half-life of neglect and decay. In the early 1980s, the trackbed from Wadebridge to Padstow was revived as the Camel Trail, a recreational route for walkers, cyclists and horseriders, while the trackbed from Launceston towards Egloskerry was taken over by the narrow gauge Launceston Steam Railway; but the rest of the route remained (and remains today) nothing more than a narrow industrial scar etched into the surface of the landscape. Parts are used as access roads for farmers; a few sections are used for grazing sheep or cattle; and most of the stations have been converted into stylish private dwellings. However, other stretches are wasted and useless, and year by year fill up with an ever more impenetrable barrier of vegetation.

The North Cornwall line thus stands as a perfect example of a railway after closure: part is now a properly constituted railway path; part now resounds again to the clank and rattle of a passing steam locomotive; while the rest is used for whatever piecemeal purpose can be devised – sometimes, nothing at all. This book is concerned with those sections of abandoned railway in the south and west of England which have been lucky enough to have been converted into official railway walks.

How much trackbed was initially available for this purpose? Some authors reckon that 10,000 miles is a reasonable estimate of the route mileage closed since 1923, although that includes tramways, colliery railways and the like; in fact, every conceivable form of rail-borne transport. How much of this total has actually been converted or made available to the public for recreational purposes? Perhaps as much as one tenth, if one stretches the definition of a railway path to include the routes of tramways in places such as Dartmoor where the public now has a general right of access. To be honest, the sum total is not impressive and ought to be a source of shame and embarrassment: if only there were some responsible authority which *could* be shamed and embarrassed by it. But that is another story, for the main drift of this volume is recreational.

A question which arises nonetheless is how exactly this tremendous mileage of railway came to be closed in the first place. Christopher Somerville, one of the earliest writers on the subject, has pointed out that our abandoned railways would stretch to Russia and back if someone cared to lay them end to end. The common answer to the question is 'Dr Beeching', regarded by many as the butcher of the railways (and by a few ideologues as their saviour) but, as always, the real story is far more complicated than any generalization can suggest. A few railways, particularly those of the tramway variety, were short-term ventures anyway, their fates inextricably bound up with the mines or quarries which they served. Most of the tramways in the Forest of Dean were of this type; as soon as their associated mineral workings were exhausted, they rapidly fell into disuse. Some were removed rapidly, especially when re-use at another site was possible, while others gradually decayed back into the ground. Some of the tramways in this category still present evidence of their existence today, one example being the moorland stretches of the Haytor Granite Tramway in Devon, where regular use ceased about 1858!

The First World War instigated the chain of events which was to kill off many rural railways, for the demands of war led to necessary and substantial improvements in the development of the internal combustion engine. After 1918, these developments could be diverted into peaceful applications, the petrol driven bus being the most obvious and damaging example. Many stations on rural branch lines were ill-sited due to considerations of geography and capital (or the lack of it), and this made them particularly vulnerable to buses which were cheaper and ran into the village centre instead of dropping passengers one or two miles distant at the top or bottom of a long hill.

A few lines were unlucky enough to be closed during the war. The East Southsea branch in Portsmouth was perhaps the unluckiest of all: competing electric trams had already stolen most of its passengers when, in 1915, it was closed, the rails lifted and reputedly melted down for the manufacture of munitions. If this last detail is correct, some of the Kaiser's soldiers must have been killed by bits of an English permanent way. The light railway from Basingstoke to Alton was another curiosity, being closed in 1917, then lifted and transported wholesale to France where it was used in the war effort. The Basingstoke and Alton really was a line that nobody wanted, for it was built to keep the Great Western Railway out rather than to fulfil any deep-seated desire of the local people for the benefits of rail travel. Despite this, the locals had become sufficiently attached to it to demand its reinstatement after the war and the trains began running again on 18 August 1924.

IVS volunteers at work on the abandoned trackbed of the Midland and South Western Junction Railway. The section from Chiseldon to Marlborough was converted into a railway path and cycle route in summer 1989

Sustrans Ltd

Some writers trace the decline of the railways to the grouping of 1923 and nationalization in 1948. They see in the latter a reduction of competition without which some duplicate routes simply withered and died. There is a strong element of truth in this, and one only has to look as far as the Midland and South Western Junction Railway to find an example. This cross-country line was a model of efficiency until the Great Western Railway got its hands on it in 1923; there was even an exodus of MSWJR staff in fear of the likely consequences. The GWR had long seen this independent line as an interloper into its territory and the grouping, whether intended or not, gave the larger company the perfect opportunity to settle old scores. Within a short time, the MSWJR shrank from being a reliable and spirited independent company to a slow and tedious secondary route.

Despite this, it would be a mistake to blame everything on the loss of competition. Before the war, a number of companies were beginning to realize that there was more to be gained from cooperation than costly, and possibly ruinous, competition, while a number of routes such as the Basingstoke and Alton had no legitimacy in terms of public demand anyway. They were purely defensive lines laid down in a political battle for territory. It is hardly surprising that the Southern Railway killed off the Basingstoke and Alton line for good in 1932, although it found fame during its twilight years in a number of films. A spectacular crash was staged on it for *The Wrecker*, while the previously insignificant halt at Cliddesden found fame as Buggleskelly in Will Hay's splendid comedy *Oh, Mr Porter!*

The war was, of course, damaging, for the railway companies gave their all to the war effort but received very little in return. Under the circumstances, little else could be expected but it left the railways with sorely depleted finances and a serious backlog of maintenance. It is hardly surprising, therefore, that the government intervened by creating four major companies which took over the operation of Britain's railways from 1 January 1923. However, the railways were not out of the woods yet, for in many areas bus competition was beginning to bite and there was the Depression of 1929 to contend with. It is no accident that a number of lines lost their passenger services or were closed altogether in the 1930s. In the area covered by this book alone, the list includes the Ruthern Bridge branch (always a mineral line), Barnstaple to Lynton, Bridport to West Bay, Basingstoke to Alton, Chichester to Midhurst, Chichester to Selsey and the Devil's Dyke branch. While this may have seemed a significant development at the time, it was nothing compared to the wholesale closures which were to follow in the 1960s.

This trend might have gathered pace but for the intervention of the Second World War, which restored the railways to a position of national importance. However, the penalty was exactly the same as during the previous conflagration – stretched resources and a backlog of maintenance. As in 1923 this had led to the grouping, so in 1948 it led to nationalization and the formation of British Railways. The advent of British Railways was by no means a bad thing, for although it brought further closures, it also brought the famous 1950s Modernisation Plan. This heralded investment in the railways on a massive scale, the most obvious result being the gradual replacement of steam by diesel and electric traction. The diesel multiple units in the west of England were a real boon to travellers inasmuch as they offered infinitely better views from their windows; one could even sit behind the driver and keep an eye on the route ahead. They certainly enabled the author to gain a full appreciation of the beauty of the lines to Looe and Bridport.

The closures still came, of course, but they generally amounted to no more than the withdrawal of lightly used rural passenger services; freight services (particularly coal) were retained. The last trains usually attracted good crowds, although it was often these mournful last passengers whose neglect had killed the services off in the first place. There were also protests, particularly in the local press, but British Railways could point to the retention of most freight services and the development of surviving lines as a result of the Modernisation Plan.

The real sea change came in the early 1960s. By this time, the railways had become something of a thorny political issue, for they were losing large sums of money each year and there was a strong feeling in government circles that 'something had to be done'. Dr Richard Beeching of ICI had served for some time on an advisory group set up by the government to investigate ways of solving the railways' problems, and it soon became clear that he had particularly clear and articulate views on what should be done with the ailing giant. As a result, Ernest Marples, then Minister of Transport, asked him to become Chairman of British Railways, a post which he took up for five years from June 1961. This was followed in March 1963 by the publication of a document called 'The Re-Shaping of British Railways', now more commonly known as the Beeching Report. Many people were astonished at the speed with which it was produced, being generally unaware of the doctor's previous involvement with, and interest in, the industry. The basic principle of the report was considered to be fair enough, if somewhat unpalatable; that one third of the network was carrying only 1 per cent of the traffic and ought to be closed.

Beeching set about implementing this policy with great energy and haste. He claimed to the end that his activities were necessary surgery rather than wholesale butchery, but some awkward questions have never been satisfactorily answered. It is particularly disconcerting that many of them are still reverberating in scholarly railway histories. Many unattractive management techniques appeared at this time, such as routing traffic away from lines proposed for closure and rescheduling timetables so as to sever long-standing connections. These policies were even applied to lines which, until Beeching's arrival, had been receiving active promotion and development as a result of the 1950s Modernisation Plan; the so-called Cuckoo Line from Polegate to Eridge is a case in point. Another problem was the fact that no means was provided for questioning the 'sometimes suspect figures produced by British Railways to support any measure they deemed necessary' (H.P. White). The underlying challenge is that some of the closures were stage-managed: the lines were going to go by hook or by crook.

It is also possible to see the old spectre of inter-company rivalry in all this. The Southern Railway's network in Devon and Cornwall became known as 'the withered arm' such was the scale of closures inflicted upon it. The closure of the line from Bodmin Road to Bodmin, Wadebridge and Padstow has always bothered the author, inasmuch as it served a substantial population along its route, and probably a greater population than exists along some of the surviving GWR branch lines in the county.

This is not the place to argue out these claims, but the whole episode ushered in a bleak period in railway history. Successive BR chairmen until Sir Peter Parker had a gloomy air about them, for they were presiding over a still declining industry and it seemed that many of their officers were too well schooled in the ways of running things down. As for Dr Beeching, he knew that posterity would regard him as the axeman, but he always argued the case of the 'careful surgeon'. The author sees him as a sort of state executioner, for that is probably what his job amounted to. If he had not accepted it, and the associated opprobrium, someone else would have done so instead. The sixties, after all, were a self-consciously modern and destructive age: private rather than public transport was the thing.

But what was done with the 6,000 or so miles of railway line which were closed and lifted? Regrettably, practically nothing. The British Rail Property Board was created in 1969 with a brief to sell off surplus railway land for the highest price possible, but as far as any re-use of the lines as recreational through routes was concerned, this was a highly destructive policy. The fact that we have any railway paths at all in the 1990s can look like a mixture of accident and miracle.

In practice, the Property Board first offered the lines to local councils. Unfortunately, their potential as recreational routes was generally not appreciated and, if the offer was made at an inconvenient time, when funds were short or other business pressing, the statutory period for the council to reply could soon pass. The plain fact is that many councils could not see much point in owning a narrow stretch of land some fifteen or twenty miles long. Some purchased old railways for possible future road improvements and it is pleasing to say that sometimes the road improvements were never necessary. Councils thus effectively 'moth-balled' the lines for long enough for some definite ideas to have developed about their re-use as recreational routes. The upshot was that a number ended up as railway paths when the original reason for their acquisition was conceived purely in terms of improved road transport. The Test Way from Mottisfont to Fullerton in Hampshire is an example.

How, then, did the idea of using old railways as recreational routes come about? In the first instance, a number of people were using them for long-distance walks anyway. Myself and several friends were undergraduates at Exeter University in the early seventies and the extent to which Dr Beeching and his successors had curtailed travel opportunities in the west of England was keenly felt. The replacement buses, where they existed, were slow and restricted one's explorations because of their limited geographical range. The idea gradually evolved of travelling by train to a former junction station and then continuing on foot. The lines to Callington, Lyme Regis, Ilfracombe and Tiverton were all tackled in this way, although the Tiverton exploration was something of a disaster. Some madness tempted the party to make this a night-time exploration by moonlight. Perhaps better visibility would have revealed that major engineering work was being carried out on the former trackbed, for the nocturnal ramblers were soon awash in some two to three feet of highly liquid Devon mud. One might say that this served them right for trespassing, but it was an isolated example inasmuch as the Property Board had not yet made a real impact on the disposal of disused lines in the area. Many of them were still largely intact and there for exploration by anyone who was prepared to turn a blind eye to the trespass issue – an opportunity now gone for ever.

On an official level, two major reports paved the way for the widespread creation of railway paths. Both, understandably, were commissioned out of concern at the largely unused resource of thousands of miles of long thin strips of land. The first was produced for the Countryside Commission by Dr J.H. Appleton, a Reader in Geography at the University of Hull; it was published in 1970 under the title 'Disused Railways in the Countryside of England and Wales'. Appleton clearly identified the main problem in BR's disposal policy, that the legal obligation on its Property Board to sell for the highest market price was resulting in piecemeal sales and destroying the continuity of routes. Unfortunately, he did not make any proposal which would halt this destruction other than to recommend that local authorities prepared plans for the re-use of all disused railways and proper regard as to how the public interest might best be served. The second report was published in 1982 by John Grimshaw and Associates of Bristol under the title 'A Study of Disused Railways in England and Wales'. This was an altogether bolder approach which really took the bull by the horns. It concluded with thirty-three separate annexes which took a number of potential routes, all largely in public ownership already, and showed in great pragmatic detail how they could be converted into safe and segregated routes for the shared use of pedestrians and cyclists. The principle at the heart of the Grimshaw approach was to create a basic path over the whole length of the route and leave the more expensive improvements to bridges and other engineering structures until the level of use really justified it. He also recognized that disused railways followed no particular 'desire line' as far as potential users were concerned and therefore required plenty of links with other paths and 'traffic generators', such as schools, colleges and places of work.

A pilot scheme was constructed along part of the former Midland Railway line from Bath (Green Park) to Bitton. Unfortunately, urban development within Bath meant that the route had to start on the western outskirts of the city but it was a great success nonetheless and has since been extended all the way to Bristol. A recent survey indicated that the route was generating something in the order of half a million journeys per annum – not bad for a redundant railway which conveyed its last rail-borne passengers in 1966.

John Grimshaw has since set up a charitable company called Sustrans Ltd – Sustainable Transport – which is subtitled The Railway Path and Cycle Route Construction Company. Its expertise has grown over the years to the extent that it has advised many local authorities as well as undertaking its own construction projects throughout the country. All the time, Sustrans is seeking to link the routes together in order to provide a comprehensive network of interconnected cycleways, segregated as far as possible from traffic on our increasingly dangerous and congested roads. Where no abandoned railway presents itself, canal and river towpaths can be used: any route which is level and segregated from road traffic is potentially usable. The company currently has a number of long-term projects, the principal ones being the creation of through routes from London to the Bristol Channel, from London to Inverness and from east to west across the Pennines. These schemes are not going to reach fruition in the next couple of weeks, but at least they are there as long-term ambitions which give unity and purpose to local projects carried out along the way; and while they may seem over-ambitious and even unlikely, one can never predict with absolute authority what may or may not happen in the future.

The construction techniques used by the company are remarkably simple, yet durable and effective. If the railway ballast is left in place, limestone dust can be raked in on top then watered and rolled in with a vibrating roller. This technique has the advantage that it is self-correcting if there is any slight movement in the foundations. Tarmac, on the other hand, simply cracks and splits, as the local authority found on the railway path from Cowes to Newport on the Isle of Wight. Construction costs in the past have been remarkably small, thanks to grants from agencies such as the Manpower Services Commission (for labour) and the Countryside Commission (for materials). Where other grant aid has been found as well, some councils have been asked to find as little as 5 per cent of the overall cost. The nett result is beneficial in practically every conceivable respect. The local authority is presented with an attractive amenity which prevents the old railway becoming a derelict industrial eyesore; British Rail is relieved of long-term responsibility for the maintenance of all engineering structures; and local people are encouraged to forsake the roads, which has benefits in terms of health and reducing accidents.

Problems are perceived as well, of course, although experience suggests that these are usually exaggerated. The main worries are loss of privacy to neighbouring properties, vandalism, crime and noise from motor bikes. The privacy issue is an interesting one, for there are cases around the country where residents, having initially opposed a railway path, finally put in gates at the end of the garden so that they can get straight onto it from their own property. In other cases, hedge planting seems to be an acceptable solution. The motor-bike problem hardly ever arises because Sustrans has developed a type of barred access onto its paths which effectively keeps out motor cycles altogether. Vandalism and crime are controlled by the fact that the routes are extremely popular and well used. On the other hand, I have found that some complainants are themselves not being entirely fair. There are cases where local residents have taken over parts of old lines for their own business purposes when they clearly have no legal right to do so: the trackbed is still owned by the local authority and the local authority is perfectly entitled to dedicate its land to a railway path and cycle route should it choose to do so.

Other problems beset the routes after their completion. A trust fund is usually set up for each individual project and this, in association with the local authority, has responsibility for long-term maintenance costs. Unfortunately, a number of other agencies may also have rights in the route. Along the Kennet and Avon Canal, for example, the British Waterways Board has a permanent right of access for canal maintenance. This is only right and proper, of course, as the cycleway is strictly the intruder, but it is a crying shame to see the state in which the BWB leaves the route when it has finished working on the canal. It is not really fair to replace a length of properly constructed cycleway with nothing more than packed earth, which is what has happened in a number of places. It is far too prone to waterlogging and rutting, which the original surface was specifically designed to avoid. Some councils have experienced similar problems with local water authorities, especially where mains or sewers have been laid beneath old trackbeds, but they are generally more responsible and constructive. In Hampshire, for example, the water authority closed the Ashley Trailway to install a new main but re-opened it with an improved surface.

On a more fundamental level, and extending the argument to railway paths generally, the ownership of the route can create management problems. Some of the earliest routes in southern England were created by councils before any clear idea had developed as to the best way to go about running them. West Sussex, for example, acquired the line from Rudgwick to Bramber in 1968, dedicated a public bridleway along it and then started to sell the land off to adjoining landowners. Such a policy would never be implemented now, for it allows the council little control over the maintenance and general state of the route. One cannot blame farmers for filling in cuttings or eradicating the railway formation where it is on a level with adjoining fields for the very sound reason that it is their property and they can do what they like with it. However, the county's ranger service is now in a difficult situation where it must somehow turn back the clock and put things right.

Generally, there appears to be a consensus nowadays that the right way to create a railway path is for the council to acquire the trackbed, lay in an appropriate surface and then allow users access on a permissive basis. This gives the council the right to close the path if, as is sometimes the case, its surface becomes so damaged that it needs to be replaced. Such damage is usually inflicted by horses cantering or galloping and the author believes that their riders should have segregated provision on railway paths, if they have to be admitted at all. There is plenty of evidence to support the case that walkers, cyclists and horseriders sharing the same surface do not mix. There is also a moral obligation on the representatives of equestrian societies to be more circumspect and self-critical. The Downs Link in West Sussex has been cited as a path on which there is no difficulty or conflict in use between cyclists and horseriders. Personal inspection suggests that the representatives of cycling organizations would probably want to challenge this claim!

On balance, however, the difficulties which occur on these routes are relatively minor and pale into insignificance when compared with all that has been achieved. Despite the fact that practically no one took action to preserve the integrity of the routes at the time they were closed, we actually have a growing network of railway paths. Some of them have been created against significant odds, particularly where the continuity of the route has been broken and extensive negotiations were required to put things back together again. The best of the paths – and that does generally mean those which have been constructed to the standards adopted by Sustrans – are immensely popular and well used, and it is to be hoped that the developments of the last ten years are just the beginning. In spring 1987, Sustrans had already completed contracts worth just under £24 million and it still had a lot of other work in the pipeline. Long may the trend continue.

So much then for the history and development of railway paths, but what can one expect to see on them? Basically, anything that once stood on the line when it was in operational use, although in much smaller quantity. British Rail, preservation societies and private collectors have seen to it that much of the peculiar technology associated with railways has been removed. However, while one may not come across many signals, point rods, pulleys and cables, buildings and engineering works are far more difficult to eradicate. A considerable number of stations survive and they clearly reflect the architectural styles of the companies which put them there. In the Cheddar Valley, there are several examples of the grand style of the Bristol and Exeter Railway; at Padstow, the station building is to a standard design used along the whole length of the North Cornwall line, that far-flung outpost of the London and South Western Railway; while at Holmsley in the New Forest, the station reflects the style of the long-vanished Southampton and Dorchester Railway.

Bridges and viaducts are the most distinctive features of abandoned railways, although viaducts are not abundant on railway walks in the south and west of England. The best place to go looking is on the Plym Valley Railway Path and Cycle Route from Marsh Mills, Plymouth, to Goodameavy on the southern slopes of Dartmoor. Frustratingly, some of the best viaducts in the area are on routes which have not been converted: Holsworthy in Devon, Shawford in Hampshire and the long succession of viaducts along the former Somerset and Dorset Railway are three examples which come readily to mind. It remains to be seen how long some of these structures will survive, given that they now serve no practical purpose whatsoever. The viaducts between Marsh Mills and Goodameavy may have been reduced to nothing more than glorified footbridges, but they are at least in regular daily use. Bridges, on the other hand, are commonplace, although a proportion of rail-over-road bridges have been demolished in order to reduce maintenance costs and improve visibility for road traffic. Bridges over rivers are always the most impressive and there are fine examples at Padstow and between Bath and Bitton. On the Downs Link in West Sussex, there is a unique 'double-decker' bridge over the River Arun between Rudgwick and Slinfold, while the Plym Valley Railway Path and Cycle Route even boasts a small aqueduct.

Tunnels are another unique characteristic of abandoned railways, although few authorities have opened them up to the public. The only examples in the area are Shaugh Prior Tunnel on the Plym Valley route; Instow Tunnel on the Barnstaple–Bideford route; Shute Shelve Tunnel in the Cheddar Valley; Staple

Hill Tunnel between Mangotsfield and Bristol; and Newport Tunnel on the Isle of Wight. The rest remain securely closed for safety reasons: a few contain dangerous drainage shafts and, where there is water seepage from above, there is a risk that bricks may become loose and fall from the ceiling.

The remaining engineering works are embankments and cuttings. An embankment can generally be relied upon for a good view of the surrounding countryside while a cutting forms a closed, secretive world of its own – often now a haven for wildlife. Those cuttings hewn through rock also hold other secrets, for the navvies' pick marks can often be traced, or the drill holes in which explosive charges were placed during the line's construction. The navvies believed that they were building the railways for good: their scratches on the face of nature can be taken as a measure of the frailty of human endeavour. Beyond all this, there are the remains of more peripheral things – fenceposts, mileposts, gradient posts, many of them now just armless stumps; telegraph poles; loading gauges; gangers' huts; sand boxes; boundary markers – all of them part of a now vanished system, as remote from modern high-speed railways as the Roman Empire.

Here, then, is the fascinating world of disused railways which this book invites you to explore. All of the routes described are officially open to the public so there are no problems with trespass. All you need generally is a pair of stout shoes and the relevant Ordnance Survey map. Armed with this, you do not even need to complete the entire walk but can return the way you came or find an alternative via footpaths and bridleways. If a particular walk needs to be done in a certain direction, perhaps due to eccentricities in local public transport, the relevant chapter will make this clear. Similar warnings are given if there are no intervening pubs or if conditions are likely to be wet underfoot. The Ordnance Survey map is also valuable inasmuch as many railway paths begin down a side street on the outskirts of town. The reason for this is not difficult to see: there is a great land hunger in our towns and cities, and central sites vacated by the railway are soon put to other uses. It is only on the fringes that the old line begins to surface again from modern redevelopment, and it is here that many a railway path begins. On a practical note, a judicious grid reference has frequently enabled me to avoid excessive directions, and this should greatly help the flow of the narrative. Wheelchair users are referred to Appendix B for the suitability of each route.

Each chapter can be read as an entirely self-contained unit and the basic pattern will soon become familiar. Should a particular walk whet the reader's appetite for more, further explorations are suggested in each locality. The basic idea was that each chapter should provide enough material for a localized week-long walking holiday focussing on disused railways and industrial archaeology generally. It was once said that there is no point in getting more people into the countryside if, when they get there, they don't know what they are looking at. It is hoped that anyone attempting a walk from this book will feel extremely well informed and, above all, enjoy themselves.

1
THE PLYM VALLEY RAILWAY PATH AND CYCLE ROUTE

Goodameavy to Marsh Mills

Introduction

When the main line from Okehampton to Bere Alston closed on 6 May 1968, the rail traveller lost his last chance to travel by train across England's most westerly national park. The surviving Great Western route from Exeter to Plymouth skirts around Dartmoor, never daring to cross its boundary, while the restored Dart Valley Railway stops at Buckfastleigh, just short of the same seemingly impenetrable barrier.

The Victorians and their predecessors were made of sterner stuff. Granite, slate, china clay and peat lured early developers such as Sir Thomas Tyrwhitt on to the moor in the belief that they could populate and develop it. The first tramway opened in 1820 and carried granite from workings on Haytor Down into the valley of the River Bovey. Tyrwhitt's own Plymouth and Dartmoor Railway followed three years later in 1823. However, many of these early lines went through periods of considerable financial leanness and this remained a problem for every railway which dared to take on the 'dark moor'. While thousands might flock there on a sunny bank holiday, the trains often ran empty at other times of the year. The geology was too barren and unyielding, the weather too harsh and unpredictable, for men to tame its great rock-strewn wilderness permanently.

Travelling west, the modern high-speed train leaves Dartmoor behind just after station-less Ivybridge. Station-less Plympton follows, where the traveller catches a brief glimpse of Tavistock Junction Yard on the north side of the line. Tavistock Junction must seem an odd name for a marshalling yard in Plymouth, but this is where the former GWR branch to Tavistock and Launceston once left the west of England main line. Through the good offices of Sustrans Ltd, six miles of this fascinating line are now in use as a segregated, traffic free railway path and cycleway from the outskirts of Plymouth to south Dartmoor. This gives the railway rambler the opportunity to do on foot what the modern passenger train may do no longer – cross the moor's boundary on a railway trackbed.

History

The first line to use the Plym Valley as a route on to Dartmoor was the Plymouth and Dartmoor Railway. The main architect of this was Sir Thomas Tyrwhitt, who had earlier persuaded the Admiralty to use the site of Princetown to establish a 'depot' for French prisoners of war. This received its first captives in 1809 but, after the 1815 peace, became deserted. Tyrwhitt then turned his attention to attracting less unwilling residents onto the moor and promoted a railway which would take out granite and peat and bring in coal, timber, lime, sea sand and the necessities of civilized life, such as tea and sugar. The line was laid to the 'Dartmoor' gauge of 4 ft 6 in and opened on 26 September 1823 from King's Tor near Princetown to Sutton Pool, just off Plymouth Sound.

The company led a precarious financial existence almost from the start and few could have been surprised when, in 1881, the section from Yelverton to Princetown was taken over by the standard gauge Princetown branch for a price of £22,000. The section from Yelverton southwards was then used only occasionally until 1900. At the Plymouth end, part of the line was incorporated into the Lee Moor Tramway but the rest of the rails were removed in 1916 and melted down for the manufacture of munitions in the First World War.

The major line through the Plym Valley was the branch from Marsh Mills to Tavistock. After years of controversy, this was finally opened by the South Devon and Tavistock Railway on 22 June 1859, an extension to Launceston following on 1 June 1865. The branch was a heavily engineered line originally laid to Brunel's 7 ft broad gauge. It included three tunnels and six timber viaducts, which were replaced with brick and stone structures between 1893 and 1910. Ramblers will be interested to discover that the tunnel at Shaugh and four viaducts at Cann Wood, Riverford, Bickleigh and Ham Green are all incorporated in the present-day walk.

The casual visitor might be forgiven for thinking that the line existed as nothing more than a rural branch, but this was not the case. Between 1876 and 1890, it also accommodated standard gauge LSWR express trains from Waterloo to Plymouth. This came about because the line's authorizing Act of 1854 empowered the Board of Trade to order the laying of standard gauge rails for use by any connecting company. The LSWR-backed Devon and Cornwall Railway took up the option when the broad gauge companies thwarted its efforts to create a separate, independent route to Marsh Mills.

Marsh Mills station on the former GWR line north from Plymouth. The stopping place here originally boasted only a single platform but was enlarged in 1894. A 44xx series 2–6–2T is seen passing through the station at the head of a train of ballast hoppers

Lens of Sutton

The resulting arrangement was rather awkward, to say the least, and gave rise to some complicated trackwork at junctions. For fourteen years, broad gauge local trains operated by the GWR were interspersed with standard gauge express trains operated by the LSWR. There was even a nightly freight working which conveyed wagons of *both* gauges – a veritable shunter's nightmare! However, the GWR always gave priority to its own trains and, while this was understandable, it was an inconvenience to the competing company which continued to aspire to its own route into Plymouth. This was achieved in 1890 when LSWR trains finally left the branch for a new line via Bere Alston and St Budeaux. The LSWR, and subsequently the Southern Railway, retained running powers over the Plym Valley line until nationalization in 1948 but it appears that they were never used.

On the opening day in 1859, the branch was provided with stations at Horrabridge and Bickleigh only. Marsh Mills was opened on 15 March 1861 and did a brisk trade in passengers for nearby Plympton market but it was not until the early years of the twentieth century that the rest of the stations were opened. Halts were added at Whitchurch and Plym Bridge in 1906, at Shaugh Bridge in 1907 and at Clearbrook in 1928. These additions were accompanied by improvements in the service and cheap fares on the Plymouth to Tavistock section of the line, which kept it busy until the start of the Second World War. Up to 20,000 passengers were recorded on bank holidays, many travelling to the popular beauty spots at Plym Bridge and Shaugh Bridge. The journey from Plymouth to Shaugh Bridge became known as a 'Woolworth trip' on account of its cheap sixpenny fare; the significance of this lies in the fact that the early Woolworth stores sold no single item at a higher price. Now that the railway has gone, the number of visitors to Shaugh Bridge has diminished, but Plym Bridge remains a popular beauty spot thanks to the National Trust, which owns and protects nearly two miles of the valley as the Plym Bridge Estate.

In 1921, china clay traffic began to run over the southern extremity of the line. Today, as on several other West Country branches, this is the only remaining traffic, with daily trips to the docks at Par and Fowey in Cornwall.

In 1939, a short branch was opened from Marsh Mills to an army depot at Coypool and this marked the zenith of railway development in the valley. On 1 January 1948, the railways were nationalized and the branch passed into the care of the Western Region of British Railways. The only immediate change was the renaming of rival stations at Launceston and Tavistock to avoid confusion but, within a few years, road competition was beginning to make serious inroads. On 30 June 1952, some rationalization was carried out by reducing the number of passenger stations at Launceston to one and then, on 5 March 1956, the branch from Yelverton to Princetown was closed completely. Two locomotives and six coaches were required to deal with the volume of traffic on that final day, but a heavy Dartmoor fog descended to deprive passengers of the splendid views.

By this time, the main branch itself was in serious trouble. The bank holiday traffic, which between the wars had peaked at 20,000, now seldom reached a tenth of that figure. Traffic on the winter services had declined so severely that many trains carried less than ten passengers each. The end came on Saturday 29 December 1962. The *Railway Magazine* reported the final day under the heading 'Inclement End to West Country Branch', an overly modest announcement which disguised the fact that appalling weather preserved the line for a further two days. The last train to get back to Plymouth on 29 December was the 5.40 p.m. from Launceston. This struggled into Marsh Mills at 7.54 p.m., where railwaymen then fought a two-hour battle to release frozen points. The train eventually arrived in Plymouth at 10.25 p.m., a full three hours late. Other trains on that blizzard-beaten day were not so lucky. The 7.10 p.m. from Tavistock to Plymouth was held at Bickleigh due to the blockage at Marsh Mills, froze to the rails and had to be abandoned. The 6.20 p.m. from Plymouth to Launceston was seventy minutes late in starting and became trapped at Tavistock, where the sixty passengers had to make do for the night as best they could. All other services were cancelled, the stranded trains at Bickleigh and Tavistock being retrieved by relief engines from Plymouth on the Sunday and Monday following.

In March 1963, a final train ran the length of the line to collect all reusable fixtures and fittings. Track-lifting south of Tavistock was awarded to a contractor who commenced work in April 1964 and completed his gloomy task in the autumn of that year. The Launceston end of the line enjoyed a brief revival when a local freight service was reinstated to Lifton on 7 September 1964, but this proved short-lived and was withdrawn for good on 28 February 1966. At the Marsh Mills end, traffic continued from the army depot at Coypool and the china clay works north-west of Plympton, but the west-facing junction with the main line into Plymouth was removed in April 1965 and replaced with a new east-facing link into Tavistock Junction Marshalling Yard. The Coypool branch closed on 31 March 1982 and this left china clay as the sole surviving traffic. It still originates at Lee Moor but, rather than travelling to the works on the Lee Moor Tramway, is now pumped there via a pipeline which runs beneath the tramway's abandoned trackbed.

And there the story might have ended but for the Plym Valley Railway. This was formed in 1980 after an unsuccessful attempt to persuade British Rail to allow Sunday steam workings on its delightful Gunnislake branch. Attention then turned to reviving steam on the Plym Valley route, initially over a relaid section from Marsh Mills to Plym Bridge. The trackbed has already been cleared and tracklaying is proceeding steadily northwards. The railway has a growing collection of steam locomotives which once worked in west Devon, together with a gigantic Beyer-Garrett locomotive acquired from South African Railways. This has a staggering 4–8–2 + 2–8–4 wheel arrangement and runs to a 3 ft 6 in gauge. This means that, one day, mixed gauge lines might once again be seen in the valley. Whether or not the new company ventures to run a mixed gauge train remains to be seen!

The Line Today

It is very much thanks to Sustrans Ltd that this route again enjoys a high degree of continuity. A number of landowners, including the Maristow Estate and the National Trust, kindly consented to the creation of the railway path which was subsequently carried out by Community Project teams funded by the Manpower Services Commission. The cost of materials was met by grants from the Countryside Commission, Devon County Council, Plymouth City Council and South Hams District Council. Negotiating with so many different agencies must have been a demanding and time-consuming undertaking, and the end product is a fine tribute to the cooperation of all involved.

The walk divides into a number of distinct sections. From Marsh Mills to Plym Bridge, it follows the course of the Lee Moor Tramway; the branch proper cannot be used here because the Plym Valley Railway intends to relay it. At Plym Bridge, the path switches to the GWR trackbed which it then follows to Bickleigh, where a short detour via minor lanes is necessary to avoid the

GWR Swindon-built 2–6–2T No. 4551 on a Plymouth to Tavistock train near Lipson Junction (east of Plymouth) on 14 May 1925

Lens of Sutton

privately-owned section around the site of Bickleigh station. After this, the path rejoins the trackbed for the final one and a half miles to Goodameavy.

The old line continues north of Goodameavy but there is no point in following it further, for a garden extension blocks the way at Clearbrook and the succeeding land is strictly private. No more of the line to Tavistock can be followed, but a large part of the nearby Princetown branch is now a footpath and some waymarking has already taken place. Further details appear in the 'Further Explorations' section.

The Walk (6 miles)

This walk starts at as remote a location as anyone could hope to find, just off a steep and winding Devon lane at grid reference 529646. In railway terms, this is half-way between the former stations at Clearbrook and Shaugh Bridge. The railway was built on a considerable gradient and the rambler who travels downhill to the south will discover that he has undertaken an almost effort-free walk.

Within a matter of yards, the old line enters a rock cutting and then plunges into the Stygian darkness of Shaugh Tunnel. This is about a quarter of a mile

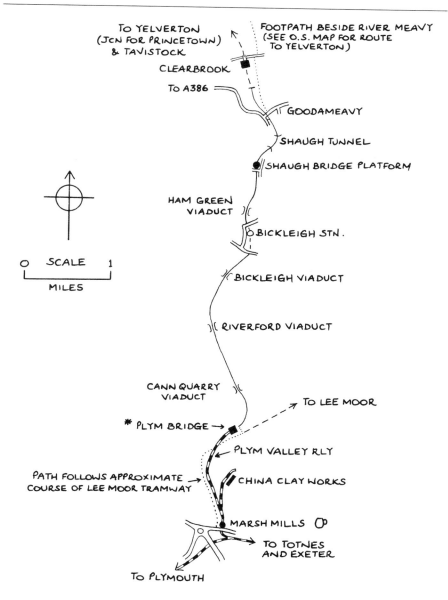

NOTES: * PROPOSED REPLACEMENT STATION
SOME DETAIL HAS BEEN OMITTED IN THE MARSH MILLS
AREA FOR THE SAKE OF CLARITY

The Plym Valley Railway Path and Cycle Route

Rail-over-road bridge at Goodameavy, just beyond the end of the Plym Valley Railway Path and Cycle Route. The very solid construction is typical of the Dartmoor railways generally

long, on a curve and a steep, descending gradient. As a result, it is very dark inside and the walker will find a strong torch invaluable. The tunnel walls have been painted white in order to improve visibility but a few years of weathering have now taken their toll and dulled the brightness. The tunnel is rather damp and water drips from the roof, especially after a period of rain – a common occurrence on Dartmoor, like the infamous cotton-wool mists. Throughout this section, the walker will notice extensive drainage works alongside and crossing the line, with culverts and channels provided to take away the water that flows down from the moor. A particularly impressive example is the iron aqueduct which crosses the line immediately beyond the south portal of the tunnel.

The site of Shaugh Bridge Platform is reached at grid reference 527637. Like stations which bore the appendage 'Road', Shaugh Bridge Platform is a good mile from the tiny village of Shaugh Prior; the designation 'Platform' suggests the spartan nature of the facilities provided here. Today, only the platform remains, overgrown with cascades of foliage.

The line continues steadily south, variously cut on ledges in the hillside, in cuttings or on substantial embankments. The view of the drop, particularly on the eastern side, is at times dramatic. The first of four viaducts is met at grid reference 525638. This is Ham Green Viaduct, notable for being the only one on

The impressive view from Ham Green Viaduct, north of Bickleigh. The stone piers to the right of the picture belonged to the original Brunelian viaduct which had a timber superstructure and was replaced in 1899

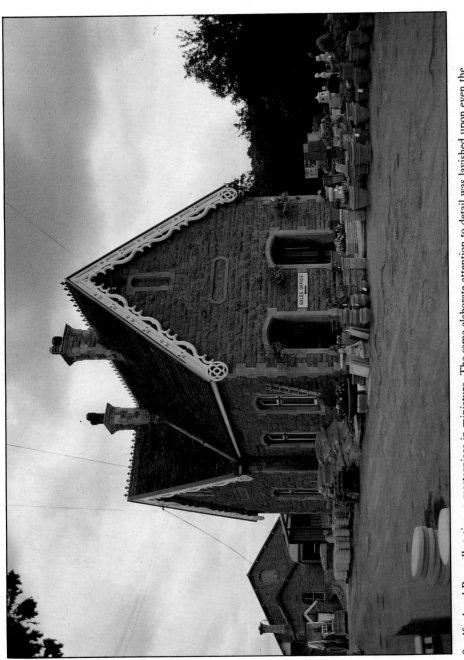

Sandford and Banwell station, a masterpiece in miniature. The same elaborate attention to detail was lavished upon even the smallest stations on the Cheddar Valley line

the line of which a good view can be obtained. The others, alas, are now surrounded by such a dense growth of trees that they are practically invisible to the outside world. If the walker looks over the eastern parapet, he will see the stone piers of the original viaduct beneath him. This was of Brunelian design, the overgrown piers originally supporting a timber superstructure. They are now believed to provide a roost for the hawks and buzzards which are often seen in the area.

Brunel's fondness for timber viaducts was well known: they must have saved the early Great Western Railway a fortune in building materials (they were presumably also quicker to erect), but the company must have had regrets when they needed replacement. The last line to have its timber viaducts replaced was the Falmouth branch in Cornwall: the replacement programme here began in 1923 but was not completed until 1934 – a surprisingly late date and perhaps some indication of the huge cost involved. The new Ham Green Viaduct was completed considerably earlier in 1899. It is an impressive structure and, like so many of these vast railway relics, stands strangely at odds with the age in which we live. A local resident remarked ruefully that it had been built in the days when man's work enhanced, rather than defaced, nature.

On approaching Bickleigh, a cutting has been filled in and the path now climbs up to meet a lane at grid reference 525625. There was once an overbridge here and the walker can get a good idea of the condition of the unconverted trackbed by peering over its southern parapet: the vegetation is so dense that nothing could get through bar a bulldozer or tank. This demonstrates very clearly the great value of the work carried out by Sustrans Ltd and its Community Project teams. The diversion here is very simple: the walker should turn right on meeting the lane and follow it to a T-junction where he turns left; the track bed may then be regained a short distance downhill on the right. This diversion bypasses the site of Bickleigh station which once stood at grid reference 526623. The Coach House, which stands on the corner of the old station approach, was once the station-master's house.

Shortly after regaining the trackbed, I met a party of disabled youngsters who were following the line for the expedition part of their Duke of Edinburgh's award. Properly converted railway paths are ideal for this sort of activity and much appreciated by those who otherwise have little opportunity to get into the 'real' countryside. Their only complaint was the lack of gated access, which meant some awkward manoeuvres to get their wheelchairs on to the main path.

Another three viaducts now follow in quick succession, Bickleigh Viaduct being the first. Like its neighbours, it provides a fine bird's eye view of the trees but the same trees make it impossible to obtain a good photographic study. Riverford and Cann Quarry viaducts are next. Cann Quarry contains plenty of interest to the industrial archaeologist and the quarry scars themselves are clearly visible on the hillside to the east of the line. Slate and elvan were once quarried here, while metallic ores were extracted from mines. All of this material was originally carried away by canal and, later, a tramway which connected with the Plymouth and Dartmoor Railway. The last slate train from Cann Quarry ran on 9 May 1855; it consisted of two horses and a few wagons.

The most obvious remains visible from the railway path are a row of derelict cottages, which must once have belonged to workers in the quarry. There is no mains water out here so they would have been very primitive by modern standards with a tub for a bath and a privy for a toilet. One of the engine drivers who worked on the branch has clear recollections of these buildings when they were inhabited. Only one family remained at that time and pretty rough they were too; hardly surprising in view of their living conditions. He and the fireman used to throw out a 'lump of coal' for them as the engine steamed past.

These could be rough times for engine drivers too, especially in winter when conditions on the footplate became extremely uncongenial. In blizzards, snow blew in through one side of the cab and straight out through the other. Tunnel work could also be hazardous. The branch had no Sunday service and this gave the water in damp Shaugh Tunnel plenty of time to form long icicles from the roof and, in extreme conditions, freeze on the rails. The first train through on a Monday morning would have to clear all this so the crew were quite used to hearing the smashing of icicles against the chimney and cab roof. On one occasion, however, the ice on the rails was so severe that the train proved unable to get through at all, even after a number of repeat runs at it. In the end, the crew had to give up and reverse back to Bickleigh, in contravention of all regulations, as they were in danger of asphixiating themselves.

Half a mile south of Cann Quarry, the railway path reaches the site of Plym Bridge Platform (grid reference 523587) just after a fine stone bridge over the lane to Plympton. British Rail removed the platform by road in 1970 and re-erected it at St Ives in Cornwall, but volunteers working for the Plym Valley Railway recently uncovered the foundations. If time permits, the walker can now visit the National Trust's Plym Bridge Estate, which comprises nearly two miles of wooded valley with footpaths, picnic areas and an information centre. It is rich in wildlife with fallow deer among the laurel and adders in the disused quarries. Young alder, oak, ash and beech trees have also been planted in order to stabilize the river banks.

The walker must now leave the former GWR line and join the Lee Moor Tramway for the final one and a quarter miles to Marsh Mills. This is achieved by crossing the National Trust's new car park, which is just below the station site and contains the only public toilets on the walk. To the north-east, a wooden bridge on a steep incline will be noted which was once part of the tramway's Cann Wood Incline. A modern pipeline has supplanted trains here but the bridge has been renewed to convey it across the lane.

Continuing south, a derelict industrial building is soon passed; this was probably a stable for tramway horses. The watercourse alongside the tramway is the former Cann Quarry Canal; its waters are usually somewhat murky but they do clear after a period of dry weather. Tramway and GWR branch run side by side for about half a mile until they cross over on the level – a most unusual arrangement; a diamond crossing in the tracks facilitated the change. The path now runs on the west side of the GWR branch, which is built on a modest embankment. The walker finally arrives at the main entrance to the Plym Valley Railway, where its South African Beyer-Garrett locomotive has pride of place.

The determined rambler can still trace the branch a little further. Just south of the Plym Valley Railway, there is a level crossing on the line to the china clay works, south of which the path can be regained. It then continues along the west platform of Marsh Mills Halt (one of the two tracks remains in place here), crosses another road and turns away to the west, following the original curve to Tavistock Junction. The path then continues to Laira Bridge on the east bank of the River Plym; it is intended in future to provide a link into the centre of Plymouth.

Further Explorations

Any walker who wishes to explore more of the Dartmoor railways should refer to Eric Hemery's excellent *Walking the Dartmoor Railroads*. This superbly accurate and thorough book provides the walker with both clear practical directions and, where possible, the names and addresses of landowners who can be contacted for permission to visit privately owned sections of old line.

The Princetown branch is close at hand and, on a clear day, can be recommended for its fine views. There is only a single obstruction from the south-east corner of Dousland (grid reference 542679) to its bleak moorland terminus, but walkers must choose their day well as precious little can be seen when the fog is down. Further to the east, the entire course of the Red Lake Railway can be traced from its terminus above Bittaford (659572) to the abandoned Red Lake china clay works (648670). The china clay itself was removed by pipeline, the railway transporting workmen and coal which was needed in prodigious quantities when the works became ice-bound in bad weather. The best clay deposits had been exhausted by 1932 and the railway was closed and lifted shortly after.

While on the subject of china clay lines, it is worth returning briefly to the Lee Moor Tramway. Part of this remained in use until 1960, a manuscript notebook found in Laira signal-box recording horse-drawn tramway workings as late as August of that year. The tramway also had two locomotives which remained unused in a shed at the north end of the line from 1947 to 1963, when restoration work began. *Lee Moor No. 1* is now at the Wheal Martyn China Clay Museum near St Austell, while *Lee Moor No. 2* is exhibited at Saltram House,

The first station north of Bideford was Instow, where the signal-box has been beautifully preserved in SR colours

Plymouth, together with a tramway wagon which was discovered in 1968 in dense undergrowth near Cann Wood Incline. It had evidently landed there after being derailed in the 1930s.

There are other railway walks elsewhere in the county. In the north, a cycle trail has been established from Barnstaple to Bideford; this starts at the existing British Rail station and makes an attractive walk with fine estuary views. The most notable remains are the station at Bideford, where the Royal Hotel still has its own imposing access onto the platform, a preserved signal-box at Instow and, again at Instow, a short tunnel which has been equipped with street lighting!

A good proportion of the Ilfracombe branch has also been converted into a railway path. The whole of this route had a very long lying-in-state during the 1970s when the local North Devon Railway attempted to revive it as a tourist line, but the company was not very prudent with its funds and the scheme collapsed. Nowadays, the railway rambler can follow the trackbed from Barnstaple to Braunton and from Mortehoe to Ilfracombe, including Slade Tunnel. Plans have been mooted to join these two sections together but it remains to be seen if anything will come of this. Barnstaple Town station, long derelict, has now been restored and converted into 'The First Class Restaurant', while the signal-box on the same site has also been restored and now houses the Lynton and Barnstaple Railway Museum.

Three other lines in the county have been preserved as tourist railways. The most famous of these are the Dart Valley line from Totnes to Buckfastleigh and the Torbay line from Paignton to Kingswear. At Totnes, British Rail passengers can occasionally witness the spectacle of a steam-hauled branch train waiting to depart from Totnes Riverside station, on the east side of the River Dart. The third survival is even more unusual, for narrow gauge electric trams now run all the year round between Colyton and Seaton on the former Seaton branch. This is the only survivor of a large number of country lines which once threaded their way to the east Devon coast from the Southern Railway's Salisbury to Exeter main line. Of such things were our holidays once made.

Transport and Facilities

Maps: Ordnance Survey: Tourist Map 1
Ordnance Survey: Landranger Series Sheet 201 (recommended)

Buses: Marsh Mills to Goodameavy is the publicly accessible part of a longer route from Plymouth to Yelverton. As a result of fierce competition between operators, Yelverton enjoys an extremely good service to Plymouth but it could prove short-lived. Walkers would therefore be wise to contact the following companies in advance:

Western National Ltd
Laira Bridge Road, Plymouth, Devon
Telephone: Plymouth (0752) 664011

Plymouth Citybus
Milehouse, Plymouth, Devon
Telephone: Plymouth (0752) 222221

Devon County Council also publishes a useful timetable booklet called 'Dartmoor Bus Services' which includes all the small local operators. For further details, contact:

The Public Transport Section,
Transport Co-ordination Centre,
County Engineers and Planning Department,
Devon County Council,
Exeter

Trains: British Rail Telephone Enquiry Bureau
Telephone: Plymouth (0752) 221300

The Plym Valley walk is rather awkward in that there are plenty of buses in the vicinity but few which go conveniently close to it and none which follow it exactly. The best approach is to take two cars for transport and a small group of friends for company; with some judicious ferrying, a vehicle can then be left at each end.

Unfortunately, this ideal arrangement will prove impossible for the individual walker, who must adopt one of the following strategies:

a. Travel by bus from Plymouth to Bickleigh, then walk south to Marsh Mills for a return bus to Plymouth. The section from Bickleigh to Goodameavy can be added if required and is only three miles there and back.
b. Travel by bus from Plymouth to the Buckland Monachorum turning just south of Yelverton on the A386 (grid reference 516671), then walk to Goodameavy using public footpaths. The path to follow starts a few yards north of the Buckland turning on the opposite side of the road. It passes under the disused railway embankment at grid reference 521670, then turns south to reach the Meavy Valley, Clearbrook and Goodameavy; a very attractive walk it is too. Join the railway path at grid reference 529646, then again head south for Marsh Mills and a return bus to Plymouth.
c. If both of these sound too awkward, hire a bicycle in Plymouth and use pedal power. For details of cycle hire facilities and a leaflet on the railway path, contact the Tourist Information Centre, Civic Centre, Plymouth.

As with bus services, so with pubs: most of them eschew the old railway line. There is no real problem in finding refreshments at Yelverton or Plympton, but these are beyond the extremities of the walk. Intermediately, only The Skylark at Clearbrook is conveniently situated. Refreshments can sometimes be obtained at Plym Bridge and, courtesy of the Plym Valley Railway, Marsh Mills, but a packed lunch is the safest bet. The railway really did 'plough its own furrow' between Plymouth and Yelverton, as these difficulties reveal all too clearly.

2
THE CHEDDAR VALLEY RAILWAY WALK
Cheddar to Yatton

Introduction

Every now and then, railway history throws significance on otherwise unlikely locations. Midhurst in West Sussex is one example and Wells in Somerset another, where three lines converged together in a lavish and arguably excessive provision of passenger facilities. Both towns are now completely without rail connections, their former lines grassy tracks gradually disappearing back into the countryside from which they were carved.

The lines to Wells came from Glastonbury, Witham and Yatton. Glastonbury, like Wells, is now totally marooned from the rail network. Witham retains a freight line which carries vast house-shaking trainloads of stone aggregate, but no passenger has boarded or alighted here since the station was closed on 3 October 1966. Yatton is the only survivor and enjoys a good service on British Rail's main line from Bristol to Weston-super-Mare and Taunton. How things change. Yatton was once a railway crossroads with branch lines to Wells and Clevedon respectively. There was a time when rail enthusiasts could travel to Clevedon and there change on to the Weston, Clevedon and Portishead Light Railway, one of the remarkable Col. Stephens' lines. This operated for many years under the spectre of bankruptcy but, when the one creditor finally withdrew his claim, neither the original nor the later railway company could be traced. This meant that the line was now legally solvent but its owners and operators had vanished. It accordingly closed down, the government of the day refusing to intervene on the grounds that 'the closing would not gravely impair the district's transport facilities', a sentiment that could not be denied.

The modern rail traveller will see little evidence of these fascinating lines from the window of his speeding HST. The best place to look is at the south-west corner of Yatton station but, even here, a new car park threatens to obscure the view. Once again, the serious railway explorer must don his boots and get out on the trackbed!

History

The history of railways in this area centres around the history of railways in Wells, for the city has long been an important centre in Somerset and, in the nineteenth century, provided a significant amount of capital used in local railway building. The first line within striking distance of the city was the Somerset Central Railway, whose line from Highbridge to Glastonbury opened on 28 August 1854. A branch to Wells was intended in the company's plans, but its construction was delayed by difficulties in raising finance. When it finally opened on 15 March 1859, the citizenry of Wells was distinctly lukewarm about being left at the end of a branch and hankered after a more direct rail connection to places such as Clevedon, Bristol and Frome. Unfortunately, the Somerset Central was equally lukewarm about extending beyond Wells due to the high engineering costs arising from steep gradients and tunnelling, so diverted its energy into plans to extend southwards to Cole where a connection could be made with the Dorset Central Railway. This was a far-reaching decision which led ultimately to the formation of the famous Somerset and Dorset Railway; the rest, as they say, is history.

This turn of events made the people of Wells very receptive to other railway proposals which promised a line to the city. The first was the East Somerset Railway, which was to be a branch from the Brunel-engineered Wiltshire, Somerset and Weymouth line. This was laid to broad gauge and left the main line at Witham, reaching Shepton Mallet on 9 November 1859 and Wells on 1 March 1862. The delay in reaching Wells was caused by difficulties in raising finance (a familiar theme in the history of the East Somerset) and the opposition of the Somerset Central Railway, which recognized the threat to its trade at Wells. In the event, this gave east-bound travellers from Wells two and half years in which to enjoy the dubious pleasures of the Shepton Mallet horse bus, which took thirty-five uncomfortable minutes to complete the bumpy five-mile journey. When the line was completed, Priory Road in Wells could boast two railway stations on opposite sides of the road; they were to remain unconnected for another sixteen years.

The last line to reach Wells was the Bristol and Exeter Railway's Cheddar Valley line. This gave the city its most direct route to Bristol and, throughout the history of railways in the area, was by far the busiest and most important. It opened on 3 August 1869 from Yatton to Cheddar, extending to Wells on 5 April 1870. The pace at which the navvies worked can be judged by the fact that these last eight miles were constructed in as many months. Intermediate stations were provided at Congresbury, Sandford, Woodborough (later renamed Winscombe), Axbridge, Cheddar, Draycott, Lodge Hill and Wookey; Lodge Hill actually served the village of Westbury-sub-Mendip but was so named to

The line from Witham to Yatton was known as the Cheddar Valley route and the station of the same name is depicted here. Originally on a broad gauge line, Cheddar station retained its overall roof to the end and this can be seen behind No. 4595 which awaits departure with a train for Yatton in the last years of the line

Lens of Sutton

avoid confusion with Westbury, Wiltshire. Wells now possessed an astonishing three stations, although they were at least arranged in a geographically straight line. From north-west to south-east, the stations were Wells Tucker Street for Yatton, Wells Priory Road for Glastonbury and Wells East Somerset for Witham and Frome. The first and third stations were broad gauge and their companies were keen for a connection, but the one in the middle was by this time part of the Somerset and Dorset Railway and had been converted to standard gauge. The history of railways in Wells is nothing if not complicated!

The ultimate solution to this, of course, lay in the conversion of the broad gauge companies to standard gauge. The East Somerset Railway was converted in June 1874, the Cheddar Valley line following in November 1875. Both companies were then absorbed by the Great Western Railway. Following this, a connection was installed between the two former broad gauge stations in Wells, the first through trains running on 1 January 1878 after the resolution of problems with the Board of Trade on the grounds of safety. This enabled the former East Somerset station to be relegated to a goods depot, Tucker Street then becoming the only GWR station in the city. Needless to say, all GWR trains sailed through the intervening Somerset and Dorset station without stopping, an inconvenience for passengers which was not rectified for another fifty-six years. This demonstrates that when the railways exercised a transport monopoly, they could more or less do as they pleased. Before we finally leave the subject of railway rivalry, it is worth mentioning an anecdote about an elderly GWR guard who was run down by a train; his dying remark is reported to have been, 'I am glad it was not one of them narrow gauge engines that did it.'

At least the three lines in Wells now had a physical connection and, following this, trade began to increase; Wells East Somerset became very busy handling goods conveyed via the S & D to GWR destinations. The main goods traffic was stone, which has long been quarried in the area, but there was a good trade in cheese, milk, strawberries, coal and even cider. The First World War gave a great impetus to the development of the internal combustion engine and lorries began to pick up the local stone movements from 1918 onwards. However, passenger traffic remained good throughout the 1920s, encouraged by cheap fares to destinations such as Weston, Burnham-on-Sea, Clevedon and Bristol. A special evening ticket was available at one shilling (5p) and this ensured that the late trains received a reasonable patronage. The only event of any note occurred one night in 1929, when the former East Somerset station, then in use as a cheese store, burnt to the ground. Road competition began to make an impression during the 1930s and forced the railway to abandon some of its more unreasonable practices, one consequence being that GWR trains began to call at Wells Priory Road from 1934 onwards. A streamlined GWR railcar also made a daily appearance over the East Somerset section from 1937, perhaps in an attempt to give the railway a more modern image. The Second World War greatly revived the fortunes of local lines and a large cold store was built at Wells with extensive sidings, which were used by the Ministry of Supply. However, when the war was over, the steady pattern of decline set in once more.

With nationalization on 1 January 1948, the whole route from Yatton to Witham passed into the stewardship of the Western Region of British Railways. Road competition and the poor siting of several stations were now having a serious effect. The first casualty was the S & D branch line from Wells to Glastonbury, which closed on 29 October 1951. In the final years, many trains were conveying only one or two passengers – hardly an economic proposition. Priory Road station was then closed to passengers, although it continued to be used for office accommodation. Wells Tucker Street was then renamed 'Wells', as it was now the only remaining station. Unfortunately, the seemingly irreversible decline in passenger traffic continued and, at the end, the only significant usage was by children attending the Wells Blue and Cathedral schools; they could easily be accommodated by replacement buses. Passenger services between Yatton and Witham were accordingly withdrawn on

9 September 1963, the final trains being packed with enthusiasts and locals bidding their last farewells. The closure notice spoke in gloomy terms of resigned acceptance: 'When considered from a logical viewpoint . . . elimination of the rail service . . . would result in a minimum of inconvenience compared with the withdrawal of road services.'

This, however, was not a Beeching closure and so freight services survived for some time afterwards; it was Dr Beeching who introduced the practice of withdrawing all facilities in one fell swoop. The closure notice allowed for a mixture of coal, parcels and freight traffic to be handled at stations such as Congresbury, Sandford, Winscombe and Axbridge, while special provisions were made to re-open Draycott station in season for the local strawberry trade. Despite this, the freight traffic was also being hit by road competition and through facilities were withdrawn on 31 March 1969, although no trains had travelled from Cheddar to Yatton for some time. Freight traffic survived over the east end of the line rather longer, most notably stone from Dulcote quarry just east of Wells and bitumen from Cranmore just east of Shepton Mallet. However, this too had petered out by the mid-1980s.

The Line Today

The extraordinary thing is that the only part of the line which remains in use today is a length of the impoverished East Somerset Railway: the first six miles from Witham to Cranmore survive as part of a freight line to Foster Yeoman's gigantic Merehead quarry. A new branch line linking the ESR with the quarry was opened by British Rail on 19 August 1970 and extensively rebuilt in September 1973. At the Cranmore end, David Shepherd, the railway preservationist and wildlife artist, opened his new East Somerset Railway in 1975. Train services began on 4 April 1980 and were extended in 1985 to a new halt at Mendip Vale, just short of Shepton Mallet. Mr Shepherd owns two large steam locomotives numbered 75029 and 92203, the latter being a member of the famous 9F class used over the Somerset and Dorset line. In a moment of apparent madness, he once used the 9F to haul a record-breaking stone train along the branch from Merehead. His success proves that the old steam workhorses can still do the work of a modern diesel.

From the end of Mr Shepherd's line to Cheddar, the trackbed is now very fragmented. A few sections still belong to British Rail, as a number of signs declare, but most of it appears to have been purchased by adjoining landowners. Some use it as a farm track while others have infilled cuttings or demolished embankments to increase the size and yield of their fields. From Cheddar to Yatton, however, the situation is rather different. After the last train had run and the track was lifted, the route was used as an unofficial footpath. The Cheddar Valley Railway Walk Society was formed in 1978 and, in that year, published a detailed and professional booklet which showed how it could be turned into an official walk. Many of the society's proposals have now been translated into fact but it is interesting to note that, for many years after closure, British Rail still classified the line as operational; the reasons for this are a mystery, unless it had an eye on future mineral extraction or the tourist trade.

The situation now is that the vast majority of the route from Cheddar to Yatton is owned by Woodspring and Sedgemoor district councils and leased to the Railway Walk Society. The section from Axbridge to Sandford is an established through walk. That from Sandford to Yatton awaits the resolution of an access problem at the Sandford end, which is currently a cul-de-sac, while the section from Cheddar to Axbridge has been approved for conversion into a cycle path.

Walk 1 – Cheddar to Axbridge (1½ miles)

Cheddar station (grid reference 455533) will probably not be included in this cycle route, but it is worth making a special trip to see it. The building has been taken over and restored to a very high standard by Wells Cathedral Stonemasons Ltd, which uses it as its base, the trackbed having been infilled to provide a large workshop area. It is hard to imagine that, in 1983, this was a mouldering ruin. The walker should note the fine stonework and decorative touches, which are a characteristic of all the surviving stations on this line. Particular features to look out for are the fine decorative woodwork, the patterns achieved in the roof tiling, the Jacobean-style chimney pots (especially at Cheddar) and the lavish mouldings in the cast-iron work; at Axbridge, these extend to lion heads moulded in the pipework. All this harks back to a lavish tradition of architecture which found its normal outlet in church-building. No one could ever accuse the Bristol and Exeter Railway of providing menial or undignified facilities at its stations!

When I visited the line, the section from Cheddar to Axbridge was impassable due to dense overgrowth at the Cheddar end. However, an official 'Cheddar Valley Railway Walk' sign was encountered half-way along the route, so some attempt had been made to open it up. The going became easier on the approach to Axbridge (grid reference 445543), where the ballast remained in place, although well bedded in. This was a delightful spot for wildlife, with large numbers of blue damselflies hovering amid the ox-eye daisies, yellow ragwort, purple marjoram and blackberries.

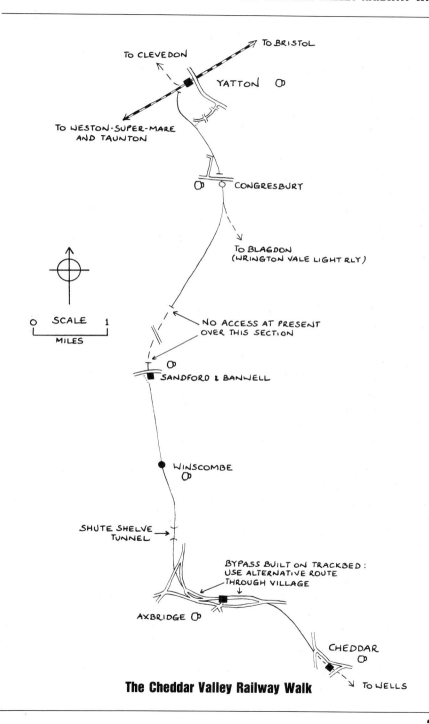

The Cheddar Valley Railway Walk

Axbridge station, now the village youth club. Note the patterns in the roof-tiling and the decorative barge-boards, both features of Cheddar stations

At grid reference 441546, a stile and a flight of new stone steps lead up to the A371, which now occupies the trackbed to Axbridge station and beyond. The walker should turn left into the old main road, which leads down to the village centre. Axbridge is pure delight, a marvellous cluster of old half-timbered buildings gathered around a market square. A market cross once stood here, unfortunately demolished in 1830; it would certainly have been restored had it survived into the twentieth century. The former railway station is now used as the local youth club and is perched high on an embankment above the thirteenth-century church (grid reference 432547).

Walk 2 – Axbridge to Sandford (3½ miles)

In 1988, the main path ran from Axbridge to Yatton and divided into two discrete sections: Axbridge to Sandford, on which there were no access problems, and Sandford to Yatton, on which there were.

The Axbridge to Sandford section starts at grid reference 424548 from the

A view of the trackbed between Cheddar and Axbridge on a misty autumn morning in September 1985. This section of the line will shortly be the Cheddar–Axbridge cycleway but it was obvious even then where the trains once ran

west end of a car park and viewpoint on the A371. This is just below Shute Shelve Hill, which the railway penetrates just under a mile later. A clear path leads down to the trackbed, which soon curves round to the north amid bellflowers and vetch, passing the occasional stumps of telegraph poles where crickets chirrup in the undergrowth. The southern portal of Shute Shelve Tunnel is reached at grid reference 422560; this was blasted through solid rock and the south end remains unlined. The walker should look for the mossy drill holes in which the explosive charges were placed; they are still there for the discerning observer. The north end of the tunnel is brick-lined and rather wet, the walls covered in mineral deposits like a lost scene from Cheddar Caves.

Winscombe station is met at grid reference 419577. The buildings have long been demolished and the site is being taken over by buddleia, rosebay willowherb and red clover. There are relatively few remains, but the determined rambler can find some old GWR iron railings, two station lamps (the second is on the station approach road) and the timber gate to the former station yard – opened for the last time years ago and now left to decay among engulfing blackberry and hawthorn bushes. This is a fairly large site and several property developers have cast wishful eyes over it, the last planning application being rejected in summer 1988. However, in today's age of land hunger and increasing development, the site cannot remain like this indefinitely.

North of Winscombe at grid reference 418583, the line appears to be blocked by garden extensions from The Grove, but the path is conveniently diverted to the left and runs behind them. It is interesting to observe the differing uses to which the occupants have put the old line; one has even preserved it, complete with pristine ballast! On approaching Sandford and Banwell station, the path swings to the left to avoid the station site which is now privately owned, joining the A368 at grid reference 415597. On meeting the main road, the walker should turn right; the station, now used as the Sandford Stone Centre, is a few hundred yards further along, again on the right. All of the railway buildings here (including the station-master's house) are well preserved. The owners are justly proud of their splendid base and, on the occasion of my visit, had rehung the roof tiles, replaced the finials and carried out much repointing of the stonework. Railway enthusiasts will be delighted to observe that everything, including the new railings, has been appropriately painted in GWR chocolate and cream livery. As the stone centre is a retail outlet, the station may be viewed whenever it is open, but walkers should respect the fact that it is private property and not stray beyond the public areas. The Railway Inn at Sandford, complete with semaphore signal, is a quarter of a mile to the east along the A368 and makes a convenient stop for refreshments.

Walk 3 – Sandford to Yatton (4½ miles)

This last section of the route is in many ways the most difficult, as the Cheddar Valley Railway Walk Society is well aware. While the old trackbed is physically clear and passes through attractive countryside, there is at present no proper access either at Sandford or Yatton station. This creates obvious difficulties for anyone attempting a through walk. While it is possible to walk from Congresbury to Yatton, the section from Congresbury to Sandford is at present a cul-de-sac and the walker must be prepared to walk back the way he came. The Railway Walk Society aims to remedy this break in continuity and continues to negotiate for a solution.

The walk starts in the middle of nowhere at grid reference 419608. Over the next one and a half miles, there have been problems with local farmers who graze animals, especially horses, on the line. Some of the horses are rather aggressive and this, understandably, deters many walkers; I met no fellow ramblers on the date of my visit, although other sections of the route were well used. This action contravenes the railway path byelaws which were signed by

Congresbury was the final stopping place before the main line was reached; it was also the junction for the Wrington Vale Light Railway which once meandered east towards the Mendip town of Blagdon. The photograph is looking south-east towards Cheddar with the junction for the Wrington Vale line in the distance beyond the signal-box

Lens of Sutton

the Secretary of State for the Environment, but the society was hopeful that measures would 'soon be taken to eliminate cattle and horses from the line'. A sad by-product of this problem has been its consumption of valuable funds in legal costs and repair work.

On the approach to Congresbury station, the Cheddar Valley line is joined by the trackbed of the former Wrington Vale Light Railway which curves in from the south-east. This ran from Blagdon to Congresbury and was a purely local affair dreamt up by farmers and big landowners who needed it to transport agricultural produce. It opened in 1901, lost its passenger service in 1931 but somehow retained a freight service until September 1963. Congresbury station has long been demolished (a pity, as it was an attractive building like the rest) but the persistent rambler can find the north ramp of the main platform if he is prepared to burrow around in the undergrowth. However, little else survives and it is difficult amid such rampant vegetation to imagine that this was ever a junction station.

Just beyond the station site, the path comes out on the A370 Weston to Bristol road (grid reference 432639). The walker should now turn left and proceed to a narrow track which heads north from the main road at grid reference 429640; this leads back to the line at grid reference 430644. The remaining one and a quarter miles to Yatton make pleasant if uneventful walking and the rambler can expect to meet a good number of local residents jogging, walking the dog or just out for a stroll. The trackbed continues right up to the former junction with British Rail's Bristol to Taunton main line, but there is no access to the station here and the development of a new station car park could make such provision rather difficult in the future. The easiest and probably only legal exit is at grid reference 426652, where a public footpath crosses the line. The walker should turn right here and follow the path into Chescombe Road, which leads directly to the town centre by Lloyds Bank. Yatton station is then just half a mile to the north.

Disregarding the need to remove livestock from the line, the improvement which this part of the walk really needs is the all-important link at Sandford which would turn it into a genuine through route. In an ideal world, access to Yatton station would also be useful but most railway ramblers know that they can't have everything. Sustrans Ltd is interested in developing the path's cycling potential, as this would introduce many more users and, without doubt, an increase in use would make livestock grazing unattractive. At the Cheddar end, the company has all the necessary agreements to develop the Axbridge–Cheddar section as a cycle path and this could provide a valuable stimulus for the route as a whole.

On the debit side, both Sustrans and local residents feel that Woodspring District Council could be rather more positive, and there is disappointment that British Rail is introducing trains on the Yatton line which have accommodation for only three bicycles, bookable in advance on payment of a fee. Perhaps Sustrans should threaten to turn the main line itself into a cycleway?

Further Explorations

There is said to be considerable local support for extending the Cheddar Valley Railway Walk towards Wells. This may take some time and could prove impracticable, but any walker who is disappointed should take himself off to Bristol and there try the fifteen miles of pioneering railway path which now occupy the old Midland Railway trackbed from Bristol St Philips to the outskirts of Bath. At Bath, a visit to Green Park station is an absolute must. This used to be a derelict hulk and was fenced off in the interests of public safety. It is now a lavish covered car park for the use of shoppers at the nearby Sainsbury's supermarket. The standard of restoration is exemplary and Sainsbury's deserve the fullest praise for their imaginative re-use of this fine building. Among other things, it houses a covered market, a pub-cum-restaurant and, on summer evenings, the odd classical concert under the cover of the train shed roof!

Mangotsfield is the half-way point and a connecting path is proposed here along the former line to Yate. At Bath, the route switches to the towpath of the restored Kennet and Avon Canal and can be followed as far as Trowbridge. Another connection is proposed here along the derelict Wilts and Berks Canal to Melksham, but the main route will continue along the Kennet and Avon to Reading, where it will connect with improvements to the River Thames towpath and provide a through route to London. Sustrans Ltd, the architects of this scheme, certainly think big. All this will take years to achieve but, in the meantime, the section from Bath to Trowbridge gives a delightful sample of things to come. This is *Titfield Thunderbolt* country and the scenery, towns and villages are quite idyllic.

Back in Somerset, the magnificent caves at Cheddar and Wookey are worth a visit. All but one of the Cheddar caves are natural and eerily attractive, the exception being an artificial cave blasted out of the rock by an amiable eccentric called Rowland Pavey. Unable to discover his own cave, Mr Pavey decided that he might as well 'invent' one. All in all, he held some unusual views, one of them being that men had invisible wings, a belief which he tested unsuccessfully by jumping from one of the smaller cliffs in the area.

On the railway theme again, we will close by returning to David Shepherd's East Somerset Railway. Some preserved lines present something of a 'Steptoe' image to the world; not so the East Somerset, which is a beautifully presented and well managed concern. Cranmore Motive Power Depot 82H is of particular note, recalling the great age of Victorian railway building. To use Mr Shepherd's own words:

We have unashamedly turned the clock backwards at Cranmore to those days of the last century. We have built a locomotive shed based on these fine traditions, which we believe is not only one of the finest in the country, but one of which the Victorians themselves would have been proud. 82H would have been the next shed number allocated if British Railways had built another steam locomotive depot in the Bristol area.

On the railway's open days, Mr Shepherd's 'giants of steam' still sit simmering outside its great wooden doors.

Transport and Facilities

Map: Ordnance Survey: Landranger Series Sheet 182 (recommended)

Buses: Badgerline
Bus Station, Beach Road, Weston-super-Mare, Avon
Telephone: Weston-super-Mare (0934) 621201

Badgerline
Bus Station, Priory Road, Wells, Somerset
Telephone: Wells (0749) 73084

Baker's Coaches
Telephone: Weston-super-Mare (0934) 636636

The main service along the Cheddar Valley Railway Walk is Badgerline service 126. This runs every hour from Weston-super-Mare to Wells via Sandford, Winscombe, Axbridge and Cheddar. A number of weekday evening and Sunday journeys are also run under contract to Avon County Council as service 826.

Baker's Coaches currently operate service 823 from Weston-super-Mare to Clevedon via Congresbury and Yatton. This is a two-hourly service which runs from approximately 8 a.m. to 4 p.m. on Mondays to Saturdays only.

All services with the prefix '8' (823, 826, etc.) are run under contract to Avon County Council. While there is a commitment to retaining the routes, their operators are liable to change depending on who, in future, submits the best tenders. For up-to-date details, contact the public transport department of the county council on the number listed in Appendix C.

Trains: British Rail Telephone Enquiry Bureaux
Telephone: Weston-super-Mare (0934) 621131/2/3
or: Bristol (0272) 294255

As can be seen from the above details, there is a 'bus chasm' between Congresbury and Sandford which will create difficulties for any rambler walking the entire length of this route. The only solution is to travel by train to Weston-super-Mare and catch a Cheddar bus there. The walker should then alight at Axbridge or Cheddar and proceed north to Yatton, where he can catch a train to complete his journey. However, do refer to the walk descriptions carefully as, at the time of writing, the Cheddar–Axbridge section had not been converted and there was no official access to the trackbed north of Sandford. Both of these problems are recognized officially and should be resolved in the fullness of time, but if in doubt, stick to the Axbridge–Sandford section and tackle the northern part of the walk from the access points at Congresbury – even if it means retracing your steps.

On the refreshments side, this is very much a holiday area and there should be no difficulty in finding a selection of pubs and cafés; all towns and villages along the route are adequately provided. Due to a devastating succession of takeovers in the 1960s, Somerset and Avon no longer possess any large independent brewers but a few pioneering companies such as the Butcombe Brewery have carved out a good name for themselves in the trade. These, as usual, are the best bet for quality and value.

3
THE FOREST OF DEAN
The Severn and Wye Railway

Introduction

The Royal Forest of Dean was Britain's first official national forest park. It occupies an area of some thirty-six square miles and is surrounded on three sides by water – the River Wye to the west and the River Severn to the south and east. The area is extremely rich in minerals and these have been exploited from Roman times. By the Middle Ages, the Forest had become Britain's main iron-working centre, although this created some conflict with the Crown: trees were being felled in order to make charcoal for iron-smelting whereas the Crown, understandably, regarded them as a national resource to be used for making warships. By Victorian times, the Forest was a significant coal-mining area. The local coal deposits were much shallower than in other areas such as South Wales and this meant that they could be exploited before the technology had been developed to undertake 'deep seam' mining. All of this placed a tremendous strain on the network of rough tracks in the Forest and plans were afoot from the very start of the nineteenth century for the construction of various plateways which would enable coal and other minerals to be removed more easily and in greater quantities. These plateways were built to take wagons with plain (i.e. non-flanged) wheels and each works used them as a public highway, supplying its own horses and wagons. The later network of railways in the Forest developed from these humble beginnings.

The history of railways in 'the Dean' is inextricably linked with the rise and fall of Forest industry. As the collieries and ironworks closed, so the railway network contracted and finally died. Nowadays, only a tiny amount of mining takes place, although there are controversial plans for opencast mining in the Parkend area; so far, none of the proposals have met with planning approval. Only a few 'free miners' keep the industry alive, working tiny pits with names like 'Strip And At It' and 'New Found Out'. These free miners are residents of the Forest who were born in the Hundred of St Briavels and have worked for a year and a day in a mine within the Hundred. They enjoy various rights and privileges which were formalized in the reign of Edward I (1272–1307) when they were recorded in the *Book of Dennis*. Apart from their mining rights, they also retain the right to graze sheep and swine. There are not many pigs in evidence but there are sheep everywhere, roaming around with unconcerned freedom like New Forest ponies in Hampshire. Disputes and threats to ancient rights are dealt with by the Verderers' Court which is held at the Speech House in the centre of the Forest.

The Dean thus has a highly individual flavour. Here is an area of outstanding natural beauty which was once one of the workhouses of Britain. Features of its local government date from the thirteenth century while the preponderance of sheep make it look different too; no trader in Cinderford dare display edible goods outside his shop! In railway days, this was the territory of the Severn and Wye Railway and Canal Company, a plucky local concern which managed for many years to keep at bay its mighty neighbours, the Great Western and Midland railways. This chapter is concerned with the history of the Severn and Wye company and the remains of its network now that the trains have gone.

History

The first proposal for a tramroad connecting the rivers Severn and Wye was made in 1799, the promoters being men of Hereford and Gloucester who wanted to reduce the cost of transporting Forest of Dean coal. Nothing came of this, but in 1809 an Act was passed for the Lydney and Lydbrook Railway. This authorized a line between the two towns with eight separate branches and allowed three years for construction. A further Act was passed in June 1810 which altered the title of the scheme to The Severn and Wye Railway and Canal Company and authorized the construction of docks and a canal at Lydney. The line was laid on stone-block sleepers to a gauge of 3 ft 6 in but this gradually widened over the years. Traffic over the line commenced in June 1810 but was stopped almost immediately as the company had omitted to install weighing machines and was conveying traffic practically free of charge. Mistakes like this are not uncommon in the company's history, often as a result of its obsession with cost-cutting; years later, it applied for permission to run passenger services when it did not actually possess any passenger vehicles. It is interesting to note that, in these early days, the line was operated very much on canal principles. The company was not a carrier and owned no horses or vehicles of its own: users were expected to provide these themselves.

Like many other local railways in later years, the Severn and Wye was under-capitalized and improvements had to be forced upon it either by disgruntled customers or the turn of events. Trade increased steadily throughout the 1820s and 1830s, but by the 1840s the line was having difficulty in meeting demand. This was largely as a result of the 1838 Dean Forest Mines Act which had authorized the expansion and modernization of local mines with a corresponding rise in output. The second incentive to modernize came from the South Wales Railway, which in 1846 applied to extend its line from Chepstow to Gloucester – a serious threat to Severn and Wye traffic. After a year of difficult negotiations which sometimes collapsed into mutual hostility, the Welsh company finally agreed to pay the Severn and Wye £15,000 towards the cost of converting its line to broad gauge. Unfortunately, after the railway obtained this money, the Commissioners of Woods made their approval of the reconstruction dependent upon unacceptably difficult conditions, as a result of which it languished in the bank for many years, largely untouched. The South Wales Railway opened its Chepstow–Gloucester line in September 1851 but the traffic interchange at Lydney revealed a great disparity between the modern railway and the ramshackle tramway.

The pressure to improve the tramway thus remained considerable and the Severn and Wye decided that, if the Commissioners of Woods were going to make it difficult to introduce the broad gauge, it might as well improve the motive power. As a result, the company obtained parliamentary approval in August 1853 to introduce steam locomotives on the line. This was followed by an inexplicable eleven year delay before the first locomotive was actually tested: perhaps the gradients were worryingly steep (they reached 1 in 40) or perhaps there were again objections from the Commissioners of Woods. In any event, when the first steam tests were carried out they were highly successful with the result that five locomotives were obtained between October 1864 and November 1865. Locomotive No. 2 was named *Little John*, and this started a tradition of naming the company's engines after characters from the legend of Robin Hood: others were called *Robin Hood, Friar Tuck, Maid Marian, Will Scarlet* and *Alan-a-Dale*. *Little John* turned out to be one of the company's most changed engines. When it was delivered, it ran on 3 ft 8 in gauge (note how the track had already widened by 2 in); it was converted in 1869 to run on broad gauge, only to be converted again in 1872 to run on standard gauge.

Notwithstanding these welcome changes, the directors of the Severn and Wye were still under great pressure to improve their line further. It could scarcely cope with the volume of traffic and the trans-shipment of goods at Lydney Junction (where the S & W met the broad gauge South Wales Railway) was regarded as a time-consuming waste of money. The directors decided to convert to broad gauge in May 1867 and accordingly had a broad gauge line installed on the east side of the existing tramway between Lydney and Wimberry, just north of Speech House Road. Most of the tramway branches faced west, so this avoided the need for many tramway/broad gauge cross-overs. The first revenue-earning freight train ran on 19 April 1869 but traffic developed very slowly because the Severn and Wye had no broad gauge wagons: customers were expected to hire these from the Great Western Railway!

Important developments now came thick and fast. The Mineral Loop, proposed in 1868, gained parliamentary authorization in 1869. This was intended to provide a number of productive collieries with a convenient outlet to the sea and represented a notable victory over the GWR and Forest of Dean Central Railway, both of which had their eye on the same valuable traffic. It would run from Tufts Junction (just south of Whitecroft) to connect with the existing line at Wimberry, running within a mile of Cinderford at its north-eastern extremity. Then in May 1870, a further Act was passed for the construction of a line from Serridge Junction to Lydbrook; this would enable the expanding Severn and Wye network to connect with the newly-opened Ross and Monmouth Railway, thus providing a northern outlet for Forest traffic. Finally, in the same month the company secretary, George Baker Keeling, ordered a broad gauge brake van from the Bristol Wagon Company. This was the railway's first item of rolling stock and in a report to the directors which was almost apologetic in tone, he explained that it was unsafe to run broad gauge trains without one.

Construction of the Mineral Loop began in September 1870 but it was converted to standard gauge before completion in line with the GWR's gauge change. The Loop was completed in the middle of June 1872, whereafter the contractors started work on the branch to Lydbrook. This opened for traffic on 26 August 1874. Both of the new lines included a tunnel and a viaduct: the tunnels were at Moseley Green and Mierystock, and the viaducts at Pillowell and Lydbrook. While the Lydbrook extension was being constructed, the company hurriedly progressed a bill through Parliament for a branch from Parkend to Coleford. The incentive was GWR competition but the Severn and Wye Bill was passed and the company rapidly constructed the new line, which opened to goods traffic in July 1875. Had it not done so, the GWR would have obtained the valuable iron ore traffic in the area.

Passenger services on the Severn and Wye commenced on 23 September 1875, the Railway Inspector having withheld permission for them to run for some three months. One important reason was that the company originally had no passenger rolling stock: this was only ordered after the Inspector's first visit! The initial passenger services were reasonably intensive but were soon cut down until by 1879 there was only train from Lydney to Lydbrook and one train on the Coleford branch.

The next major date in the railway's history was 21 July 1879, when an Act of Parliament authorized the amalgamation of the Severn and Wye Railway with the Severn Bridge Railway. The Severn Bridge Railway had been authorized in July 1872 and had intended to link Sharpness on the south bank of the Severn with Lydney on the north bank by means of a gigantic bridge across the estuary. The complicated trail of events which led to the amalgamation is beyond the scope of this book, but suffice it to say that the Midland Railway was involved and obtained running powers over the combined network as a result. The Severn Bridge finally opened for traffic on 17 October 1879 but, by then, the Severn and Wye had already suffered its first loss of independence.

The years that followed were extremely bleak ones. The spate of improvements throughout the 1870s had stretched the Severn and Wye's financial resources to the limit and it desperately needed a period of consolidation and good trading. What it received instead were years of poor receipts caused by depressed trade in the Forest, debilitated by foreign competition and damaging miners' strikes. Then in 1886, the Great Western Railway opened its famous Severn Tunnel which offered a faster through route than the secondary line over the Severn Bridge; things looked bleak indeed. By 1893, the company's locomotives were in as bad a state as its finances and, in August that year, it went into voluntary receivership. The following month, the tide suddenly turned with the start of a prolonged miners' strike in Derbyshire. Forest mines that had been closed for years were re-opened and a traffic boom descended upon the railway, now too run down to handle it properly. The directors had no funds with which to put the ailing concern back on its feet and were forced to sell out to the Midland and Great Western railways, which bought the company in 1894 for £477,300. Thereafter, the Severn and Wye network was run by a joint managing committee which remitted funds to its respective owners.

Following the purchase, the MR and GWR provided much needed replacement locomotives and rolling stock in 1895. The Act authorizing the sale also required the construction of a line into Cinderford, which the old S & W had never catered for properly: it had provided three successive stations, each one nearer the town than the last, but had never failed to provide Cinderford passengers with a long walk. This was remedied on 2 July 1900 when a new line into the town was officially opened together with a new station that was a more fitting terminus to the main line from Lydney. For all this, it was still situated at the foot of a long hill from the town centre! The Forest lines were now at their peak of development and, following another Dean Forest Mines Act in 1904, business developed extremely well, especially on the freight side.

The First World War and the 1923 grouping came and went with little obvious impact on the network, but the times ahead were very lean due to economic factors such as reduced colliery output. In 1922 and 1927, the Severn and Wye lines actually made a loss and, between the same two years, passenger receipts practically halved due to road competition. The management committee felt that the withdrawal of passenger services would have the greatest effect in reducing the railway's costs and accordingly axed all but one of them on 6 July 1929; the exception was the passenger service across the Severn Bridge. Fortunately, coal traffic began to increase at this time and this prevented the implementation of other planned economies. The management committee was

The end of the Severn Bridge Railway. One of the mighty girders from this important railway-crossing is laid to rest on the banks awaiting the attention of the cutter's torch

'R.A.' Collection

then able to settle down to dealing with its lucrative mineral traffic, unencumbered by the inconvenience of timetabled passenger trains.

This situation remained stable until the Second World War, when the Forest was used as a huge covered ammunition dump. Moseley Green Tunnel on the Mineral Loop was requisitioned for ammunition storage while other military depots were established at Acorn Patch (again on the Mineral Loop), Speech House Road and Parkend. Acorn Patch was the busiest depot and soon had eighty wagons in and out per day. Train crews recall it being in use twenty-four hours a day and having to work extra trains there after the end of their normal shifts. In fact, the military use of the Mineral Loop was its salvation, for by 1940 only one colliery along its course remained open. This closed in 1944 and thereafter the military depot was the only reason for retaining the line, but this closed as well in 1949.

After the war, trains continued to run along the northern sections to Cinderford and Lydbrook but there was often no traffic to collect and the engines ran out and back with nothing but a solitary brake van. Common sense began to prevail in 1956, when first the line from Serridge Junction to Lydbrook was closed and then the whole of the Mineral Loop. The branch from Lydney to Lydney Docks was closed in 1960 and, in the same year, passenger services across the Severn Bridge came to an abrupt end when the petrol tanker *Wastdale* collided with it in fog, bringing down one of the central piers and both adjoining spans. A passenger train had crossed only minutes earlier. By 1963, the only sections remaining in use within the Forest were Lydney Junction to Speech House Road and Parkend to Coleford and Whitecliff Quarry. Still the decline continued. The National Coal Board closed its last Forest colliery in 1965 and, by 1973, only a four-and-a-half-mile single-track branch remained from Lydney Junction to Parkend. This handled substantial tonnages of coal and ballast but, in May 1976, this traffic ceased as well. The track was retained with minimal maintenance in case of a resumption of traffic but this never occurred and, in late 1980, British Rail finally declared the section closed. Fortunately, the Dean Forest Railway Preservation Society had become established in the Forest by this time and it now started negotiations to purchase the line; a contract was finally signed and exchanged in December 1983. A Light Railway Order was then applied for and finally agreed and granted in mid-1985 following negotiations with the local authorities. Much work remains to be done in restoring the line to passenger standards but it seems highly likely that a part of the Forest will again resound to the whistle of a steam engine panting up the steeply graded branch from Lydney Junction. If proposals are finally approved for opencast mining in the Parkend area, the revived railway could even find itself with a valuable freight traffic.

During the evening of 25 October 1960, the Severn bridge was damaged beyond repair by a vessel out of control on the river, although it was not demolished until 1965. A giant floating crane is seen here ready to start work on the removal of the girders

'R.A.' Collection

The Lines Today

More than thirty years have now passed since some of these lines closed, but many can still be traced and those that are used as footpaths or bridleways will present the walker with few difficulties other than negotiating the occasional road. The Forestry Commission continues to 'run' the Forest as agent for the Crown and allows a general right of access on foot. One of the ways in which the walker can exercise this right is by exploring old railways in the area, but it goes without saying that this does not extend to climbing over fences or entering land which is obviously private. However, having said this, the walker will be pleased to discover that many stiles have been installed (e.g. on the Mineral Loop) even though their use by pedestrians is probably light.

Very little remains of the lines generally other than the trackbeds, earthworks and a small number of bridges. Most of the mileposts and gradient posts have been removed ('generally into better care than Nature affords', as railway historian Harry Paar neatly put it) while all of the tunnel portals have been sealed in the interests of safety. Lydbrook Viaduct was dismantled in 1970 and the author found no trace of Pillowell Viaduct, which must presumably have suffered the same fate.

If this presents a seemingly dull picture, the walker should remember that, theoretically at least, he can explore any dismantled plateway, tramway or railway that takes his fancy. Even the most ordinary looking Forest footpath could follow the course of some long abandoned trackbed. Writers refer lightly to the 'maze' of lines which once ran through the Forest: in places it can seem like a bewildering jungle. Some of Harry Paar's maps have to be seen to be believed, especially that of the Cinderford area. On a humorous note, tribute must be paid to the sheep which keep many tracks clear by eating anything that grows, while more seriously, the author would like to record his thanks to those helpful locals who explained which line went where and, quite literally, put him on the right track.

The Walks

These walks are described in separate sections so that ramblers can piece together a route to suit their own particular needs or interests.

Walk 1 – Parkend to Drybrook Road (4½ miles)

This is very much the main railway path within the Forest. It starts just north of Parkend at grid reference 612088, where an infilled bridge once carried the B4234 Parkend–Lydbrook road over the line; the old railway heads off to the north as a clear grassy track. In just under a mile, its enclosed woodland character changes on arrival at Cannop Ponds. The Bicslade Tramroad joined the line here: this remained a horse-drawn plateway until its final closure in November 1946. The picturesque ponds were created in 1825 when the Forest of Dean Iron Company turned an embankment on the branch into a dam in order to drive water-wheels. Nowadays, anglers wait hopefully with their rods and nets, no doubt oblivious to the fact that they owe their sport to an old tramway.

From Cannop Ponds to Speech House Road (grid reference 611117), the line is used as a rough access road from the B4226 and can be rather dusty in dry weather. Nothing remains of Speech House Road station and it is difficult to imagine the site in its heyday. On the south side of the road, there was a short branch to a wood distillation factory while, on the north side, the Howlers Slade

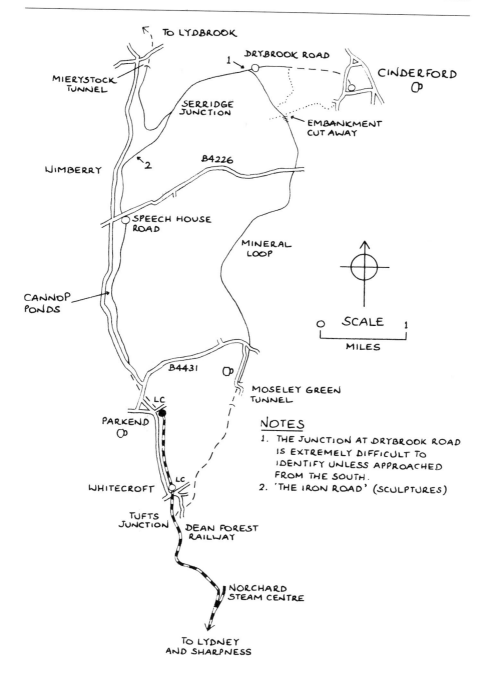

TO LYDBROOK

DRYBROOK ROAD

CINDERFORD

MIERYSTOCK
TUNNEL

SERRIDGE
JUNCTION

EMBANKMENT
CUT AWAY

WIMBERRY

B4226

SPEECH HOUSE
ROAD

MINERAL
LOOP

CANNOP
PONDS

SCALE

MILES

B4431

MOSELEY GREEN
TUNNEL

LC

PARKEND

NOTES

1. THE JUNCTION AT DRYBROOK ROAD
IS EXTREMELY DIFFICULT TO
IDENTIFY UNLESS APPROACHED
FROM THE SOUTH.

2. 'THE IRON ROAD' (SCULPTURES)

WHITECROFT

LC

TUFTS
JUNCTION

DEAN FOREST
RAILWAY

NORCHARD
STEAM CENTRE

TO LYDNEY
AND SHARPNESS

The Forest of Dean

'The Iron Road', a series of sculptures carved out of sleepers on the main line north of Speech House Road Halt

tramroad led off to serve a plethora of mines, quarries and foundries. It even served a chemical works! The main line continues its steady climb northwards past New Beechenhurst Inclosure until a fence with a stile blocks the way; beyond this lies 'The Iron Road', a set of twenty wooden sculptures made from railway sleepers laid out along the trackbed. These are part of the Sculpture Trail, which actually starts opposite Speech House. The trail is the creation of the Forest of Dean Sculpture Project, organized by the Arnolfini Gallery in Bristol in collaboration with the Forestry Commission. The response to these sculptures has been extremely good, even from those who might not expect modern sculpture to appeal to them. Railway ramblers will be particularly drawn to the wheel of fire, which seems an appropriate symbol of the Forest's industrial past.

At grid reference 619137, the Lydbrook line comes in from the north at the now empty site of Serridge Junction. The trees have grown here over the years, as old photographs reveal; it is scarcely recognizable as the neatly trimmed setting of railway days. The trackbed then enters a shallow cutting with stone retaining walls on either side, culminating in a rather unusual tunnel which

The departure platform at Nailsworth station – a far cry from the crowded Victorian photographs taken on the opening day in 1867

Bridge over the River Kennet at Marlborough

could almost be described as a long bridge (grid reference 624143). It has an extraordinarily shallow roof but there does not appear to be a track over it, which is probably just as well! Perhaps it has something to do with a nearby disused mine.

The site of Drybrook Road station is met at grid reference 633145. Nothing remains of this today, but a road crossing alerts the walker to the fact that he has arrived. Drybrook Road was the first station for Cinderford, but the Severn and Wye was taking terrible liberties here with its station naming. For a start, the 'Road' was probably nothing more than a muddy track and it gave direct access neither to Drybrook nor Cinderford; small wonder that Cinderford residents complained for years about the railway's failure to provide for them properly. On the north side of the trackbed, Brain's Tramway ran parallel to the Severn and Wye, serving a number of local mines which, according to a passing local, were the first to use electric detonators. This is also the site of the junction between the Mineral Loop and the Cinderford extension, so the walker can now either turn south along the Loop or follow the Forest paths to Cinderford; further details are given below.

Walk 2 – Moseley Green to Drybrook Road (4½ miles)

I had hoped to follow the Mineral Loop all the way from Pillowell but a visit to the section south of Moseley Green Tunnel was rather unpromising; most of the line is in a cutting which is badly overgrown with bracken – certainly not the sort of terrain for a casual afternoon walk. It is best, therefore, to start from the north portal of the tunnel which is located at grid reference 633084; a minor lane runs close by. There is a good view of the trackbed from above the portal and the walker will find a path leading down to it along the eastern side of the tunnel cutting. Shortly after joining the line, the walker will notice that the position of the sleepers can still be seen from patterns in the grass. Thanks to the healthy appetite of the local sheep, the trackbed has the appearance of a well tended lawn; it is difficult to believe that it closed as long ago as 1956.

It is a very easy walk as far as the B4431, where an underbridge has been demolished (grid reference 634091) but there is an easy path down the embankment, which is quite high at this point. The line can be regained on the other side of the road without undue difficulty, but it is rather overgrown for a few hundred yards until suddenly clearing to provide a delightful grassy trail in a secluded woodland setting. The grass is several feet high in summer and the sensation is rather like walking through an old-fashioned meadow. Fences cross the line in places but stiles are always provided. At grid reference 629108, a large bridge has been demolished but steps have been provided down one side of the embankment and up the other. A few hundred yards further on, another large bridge is still intact; it makes an impressive sight with its attractive stonework. By the time the path reaches the sawmill just south of Dilke Memorial Hospital (grid reference 641120), it has become very secluded although enough walkers use it to have frightened away the inhabitants of a large rabbit warren on the east side of the formation. There are several old industrial buildings dotted around the sawmill, plus a number of spoil tips from disused mines – one of the few visible and obvious reminders of the Forest's industrial past.

Another fine stone bridge carries the B4226 over the line at grid reference 642126, but the next section is rather damp and obstructed by fallen trees; their roots cannot get a hold in the embankment sides and they have toppled in high winds or under the weight of winter snow. Fortunately, most of them are relatively young conifers which have grown with very few branches in their struggle to reach the light, so they are not particularly difficult to get over. After this, the going becomes easy for the final run into Drybrook Road. The only minor problem is just north of Crabtreehill Plantation, where there are industrial workings which have used part of the line as a lorry road (grid reference 640137). All the walker need do is keep going straight ahead.

Taken as a whole, this walk is slightly more demanding than that from Parkend to Drybrook Road but it can still be achieved without undue difficulty. It is generally more attractive in the sense that it appears to be a wilder place which the rambler is exploring for himself. The engineering works are also more substantial, which indicates the one-time importance of mineral traffic on the line while demonstrating how the Severn and Wye got itself into financial difficulties in the 1880s. Fungi flourish in the damp cuttings, while rabbits, sheep and grey squirrels dart away on hearing the walker's approach. The warning bleats of the sheep are echoed by others unseen deep within the Forest and the walker is soon surrounded by a cacophony of bleats, all at different frequencies. Unfortunately, most of the trees along the walk are conifers which means that the forest floor is rather dead save for the ubiquitous bracken; only the old railway affords any real variety by offering a narrow slither of daylight and grass in which wild raspberries, brambles and foxgloves can become established.

Walk 3 – Mierystock to Drybrook Road (2½ miles)

This can fairly be described as an advanced ramble which requires some expertise. It does, however, have the rare distinction for the Forest of being on a regular bus route from Cinderford (Red and White's service 31). The main problem is finding the right track to follow from the start, for Mierystock is another Forest location which once possessed a tangle of railway and tramway lines. I was assisted by a very helpful and well-informed local who, *inter alia*, directed me to the south portal of Mierystock Tunnel; unfortunately, the trackbed here was waterlogged, standing in a full twelve inches of muddy water. However, the rest of the route is dry.

The bus from Cinderford to Coleford follows the A4136 Gloucester–Monmouth road. The walker should watch out for The Swan public house at

The southern portal of Mierystock Tunnel. In practice, this is not a good place to start walking as the tunnel is sealed at both ends and the trackbed stands in some 12 in of water

Brierley and alight at Mierystock crossroads, which is just under a mile further west; this is where the main road crosses the B4234 from Lydney to Lydbrook. Even the Ordnance Survey Leisure Map does not do full justice to the abundance of tracks and paths in this area, so no better advice can be offered than to seek out the tunnel portal and then head south. Mierystock Bridge still stands a few hundred yards south of the tunnel but walkers should note that the old railway ran under this; the path above is nothing more than a Forestry Commission track.

South of Mierystock Bridge the railway, and the tramway which predated it, both run parallel, the tramway keeping just to the west before entering a tunnel at grid reference 613141. The walker should follow the tramway past an overgrown section of the railway and then switch left onto the main trackbed. The line then heads south for half a mile before entering a long horseshoe curve which sweeps around the southern slopes of Serridge Inclosure. Serridge Junction is met at grid reference 619137 and the walker can then continue east to Drybrook Road, as described in Walk 1 above.

Walk 4 – Drybrook Road to Cinderford (1½ miles)

This is not a railway path as such but the essential link route which enables walkers to make their exit from the secluded world of the Forest railways. It is worth noting that recent alterations to local roads and Forestry Commission trails have not found their way onto the Ordnance Survey maps published in 1985 and 1987.

Walkers should continue east from Drybrook Road until meeting an earth mound across the trackbed. Turn right here and join a wide, well-made dirt track. Follow this for approximately three-quarters of a mile to a crossroads of tracks and there turn left; Cinderford may now be seen straight ahead through a gap in the trees. Follow the path downhill until it joins a metalled road in the valley below the town. Turn left here and then right at the roundabout which follows in 75 yds. You are now in Valley Road, Cinderford. Station Street is about 400 yds along on the right and leads uphill to the town centre. The site of Cinderford station is passed on the left, marked by a plaque for 'The Keelings', a new housing development which stands where local trains for Lydney and Newnham once waited for the off. The English is rather jerky but it tells the tale:

Site of Cinderford Railway Station 1900–1968
Opened by the Great Western & Midland Railway Companies

Joint Severn & Wye & Severn Bridge Railway
George Baker Keeling 1804–1894 and his
son George William Keeling 1839–1913
Railway Engineers who were responsible for bringing
the railway through the Forest of Dean to Cinderford

It is to the credit of the developers that they have done their homework and come up with a name which has real local significance. One gets rather tired of variations on the over-common 'Beeching Close'.

Further Explorations

Outside the Forest, the only other public access to a former railway in the area is along the Wye Valley Walk, which utilizes just under three and a half miles of the former Chepstow to Monmouth line but not, alas, in one contiguous length. However, it does include the old station at Tintern, which has been beautifully restored as a picnic and exhibition centre. The Wye Valley Walk starts in Chepstow and follows the river north for thirty-four miles to Ross-on-Wye, so it is not a journey to be undertaken lightly.

On the railway preservation side, mention has already been made of the Dean Forest Railway which is based at Norchard, about a mile north of Lydney. The company is purchasing the four and a half miles of track from Lydney to Parkend and hopes to restore a passenger service along the branch in the fullness of time. It is under no illusion about the amount of work involved but the restoration of such a service, even on a seasonal basis, would greatly improve access to the Forest and its railway paths. The railway has already restored a number of locomotives and coaches, including two distinctive GWR auto-trailers. As is so often the case, many other vehicles await restoration but there are some interesting items in the pipeline, not least a set of four pre-war GWR coaches which were converted in 1962 into a mobile telephone exchange for use by the Ministry of Defence in an emergency. After conversion, they were stored at a secret location near Craven Arms until disposed of in 1981. When they have been restored, they will make a fine addition to the railway's working stock.

A more recent and therefore less well-known enterprise is the GWR Museum at Coleford. This is based in an attractive site around the old GWR goods shed, which has been painstakingly restored by the proprietor Mike Rees with assistance from members of his family and a number of local enthusiasts. It took a 2,000 signature petition to persuade the local council that the old building was worth saving instead of razing to the ground, as it proposed in February 1984. Considering its relatively small size, the museum accommodates a considerable amount of material, collected by members of the Rees family during 107 years of local railway service. Mike's grandfather, George Ward Rees, worked for forty-five years as a signal fitter for the Midland Railway; his father gave forty-eight years of service as a cleaner, fireman and driver; while Mike himself worked for fourteen years as a railway telegraph man. He even serviced the telephones in his own goods shed! Near the end of his railway career, he took a job at Cinderford instead of moving to Reading to learn colour light signalling. This effectively sealed his fate, for in 1964 the railway started closing down. By then, railwaymen could no longer expect to give service in their own local community; it had become a case of 'move on or go'.

Transport and Facilities

Maps: Ordnance Survey: Landranger Series Sheet 162
Ordnance Survey: Outdoor Leisure Map 14 (recommended)

The Landranger map is unsuitable for tracing old railways in the Forest as many of the trackbeds are no longer shown; this is hardly unreasonable as there are so many of them! However, the Outdoor Leisure map shows all the dismantled railways with great clarity.

Buses: Red and White
Albion Square, Chepstow, Gwent, NP6 5DA
Telephone: Chepstow (029 12) 2947

Minor Operators:
a. M.S. Nash
   Telephone: Dean (0594) 33104
b. Soudley Valley Coaches
   Telephone: Dean (0594) 22129
c. Willetts of Yorkley
   Telephone: Dean (0594) 562511

For an overview of current services, contact Gloucestershire County Council on the telephone number given in Appendix C.

Trains: British Rail Telephone Enquiry Bureaux
Telephone: Newport (0633) 842222
       or: Bristol (0272) 294255
       or: Gloucester (0452) 29501

The Royal Forest of Dean is not well served by public transport and most visitors can be forgiven for arriving by car. However, if public transport must be used, there are two main routes of access:

a. Travel by train to Lydney, walk to Lydney bus station and there take a bus to Parkend, or;
b. Travel by train to Gloucester and there take a bus to Cinderford.

The Gloucester route is by far the more convenient as the bus and train stations are situated within a short walk of each other. British Rail's Lydney station is the old Great Western Lydney Junction, a full mile from the bus station in the centre of town. It is also served by only one train every two hours, which compares badly with the wide range of local and inter-regional services calling at Gloucester.

The main bus route through the Forest is Red and White's service 31. This runs from Gloucester to Cinderford and Coleford every hour Mondays to Saturdays with a couple of journeys on Sunday afternoons and evenings. A variety of minor operators make up a modest service from Lydney to Parkend: five return journeys on Mondays to Fridays, two on Saturdays and none on Sundays. Current details can be obtained from Gloucestershire County Council (see Appendix C).

There is only one service which follows any of the railway walks described below, and that is Red and White's service 32 from Chepstow to Cinderford. This runs once a day Mondays to Fridays only for the benefit of students attending West Gloucestershire College at Cinderford: it leaves Chepstow at 7.30 a.m. and returns from Cinderford at 4.30 p.m., calling intermediately at Speech House, Parkend, Whitecroft and Lydney. There are minor revisions to the timings out of term. While this could not be described as an intensive service, it does enable walkers who have followed the old railway from Parkend to Cinderford to get back to their start point.

Another solution would be to make an anti-clockwise circular walk from the north side of Moseley Green Tunnel to Parkend via the Mineral Loop and the old 'main line'. This takes in Drybrook Road, Serridge Junction, Speech House Road, Cannop Ponds and Parkend. The two ends of this walk are just under two miles apart and provide a circular walk of eight and a half miles, or ten and a half miles including the road walking between the two ends. If this is attempted, it is *essential* to walk the route anti-clockwise in order to avoid 'missing the turn' at Drybrook Road: the junction here is not at all obvious and will certainly be missed if approached from the other direction.

As for refreshment stops, there is a pub on the north side of Moseley Green Tunnel (marvellously convenient) and another at Parkend; intermediately, there is nothing unless the walker makes a time-consuming detour into

Cinderford. During holiday periods, especially at weekends, an ice-cream van may be encountered at Cannop Ponds but, taken as a whole, the facilities are few and far between so a packed lunch is a sensible precaution.

Finally, two words of warning about walking in the Forest. First, if you have to use public transport, make absolutely sure that it is still running; and second, take great care when map-reading, especially off the main path from Parkend to Drybrook Road. The network of tracks and footpaths in the Dean is probably as intricate and confusing as the maze of tramways and railway lines which preceded it.

4
THE STROUD VALLEYS PEDESTRIAN CYCLE TRAIL

Nailsworth to Stonehouse

The branch line to Nailsworth (now the Stroud Valleys Pedestrian Cycle Trail) was constructed by the independent Stonehouse and Nailsworth Railway but taken over by the Midland Railway in 1878. As such, it became part of the London, Midland and Scottish Railway with the grouping in 1923.

This being the case, its description strictly belongs in *Railway Walks: LMS* of this series, but it has been included here for obvious geographical reasons. Similarly, a GWR branch line in the Birmingham area appears in the LMS volume.

Introduction

It is tempting to think of the Cotswolds as a rustic retreat of stone cottages and skilled artisans, where honest craftsmen still make a decent living from centuries-old trades. This view owes much to William Morris' Arts and Crafts movement which flourished in the nineteenth century as a reaction to the uniformity and artlessness of manufactured products. However, for all that, the western edge of the Cotswolds around Stroud itself accommodated an important manufacturing industry, albeit one which did not scar the area with spoil tips and worked-out pits. The Cotswolds, of course, are famous for sheep and Stroud flourished on the woollen industry that went with them. Nowadays, mass production, man-made fibres and imports have all reduced the industry to the merest shadow of its former self and only two mills are still fully operational as woollen mills. Yet the industry's decline has bequeathed a legacy of dignified and characterful industrial buildings such as numerous mills and the extraordinary round teazle tower which survives at Frogmarsh near Woodchester; teazles were used to raise the fibres of the wool and local teazle merchants made a living by supplying them to manufacturers. Surprisingly few mills have been demolished, the preferred choice being to convert them into units for small businesses or, to a lesser extent, into residential accommodation.

The Great Western Railway enjoyed a monopoly on wool and other local business until a homegrown concern entitled the Stonehouse and Nailsworth Railway Company came upon the scene. In many respects, this was another case of great expectations much reduced by reality, although the reality – particularly in the form of trade depressions – was often beyond the railway's control. Despite everything, the branch was built and hung on to its existence until 1966, but it is something of a backwater which appears to have been overlooked by the majority of railway historians. Even the neighbouring branch line to Dursley, a modest affair of some two and a half miles, can boast a booklet on its history but the Nailsworth branch has to make do with the briefest of references which sometimes reduce its entire history to a mere paragraph or two. As a result, the following narrative draws heavily on the few available printed sources and acknowledgement is given to their respective authors.

History

The earliest plan for a railway between Stroud and Nailsworth was formed in the 1850s, but its bill was defeated by local MPs who wished to protect the local Turnpike Trust which obviously feared railway competition. As a result, the scheme went into hibernation and re-emerged in an enlarged form in 1861, by which time the residents of Nailsworth and nearby Tetbury had devised a plan for a through route from Stroud to Chippenham with Nailsworth as the 'railway centre' of the line. The railway was a purely local concern so a project of this magnitude would have created considerable difficulties in raising the necessary finance, not to mention the risk of antagonizing the GWR – a difficult and intractable opponent, as other chapters in this book reveal. It is probably just as well that this grandiose scheme was reduced in 1862 to a single track branch line from Stonehouse to Nailsworth. In this form, the railway's bill was passed on 13 July 1863, four years being allowed for its construction. The branch line from Dudbridge to Stroud was not applied for until 1864 although it was never built by the original company; it is not surprising, therefore, that it always bore the appearance of an afterthought.

The railway's construction was inaugurated on 27 February 1864 amid celebrations and festivities on a grand scale; these ranged from a dinner for 120 gentleman guests to musical entertainments, a torchlit procession and even bursts of cannon fire. The Revd Mills of Nailsworth blessed the railway site and the Rt Hon. A.E. Horsman, MP for Stroud, turned the first sod with a ceremonial silver shovel. However, the launch was rather extravagant in

Not to be confused with the GWR station at Stroud, this is Stroud Midland, from which a shuttle service operated to the next station on the line at Dudbridge

Lens of Sutton

comparison with what followed. The company ran into construction difficulties, the worst of which attended the skew bridge over the Stroudwater Canal at Ryeford; subsidence problems here caused serious time delays and damaging compensation claims. The line opened for goods traffic on 1 February 1867 and for passenger traffic three days later, but by this time the company was financially weak. It had failed to raise sufficient capital; no interim dividends had been paid; and it had not constructed a branch line into Stroud, which had long been the main industrial centre of the area. The company therefore found itself heavily in debt and relied increasingly on the Midland Railway, which had been contracted to provide the services from the very start. In November 1867, it turned to the Midland for major assistance but had to resort to the protection of the official receiver when this was refused.

The Stonehouse and Nailsworth Railway continued in these straitened circumstances for just over ten years until, in the late 1870s, the Midland assumed almost complete control and then absorbed it by an Act of 1 July 1878. By all accounts, the larger company had now invested considerable resources in the line and takeover was seen as the only alternative to closure. An important condition of the Act was that the extension from Dudbridge to Stroud should be built as soon as possible and powers to construct it were granted in 1880. The line was opened to goods traffic in November 1885 but construction was not completed until March 1886 and, even then, the inauguration of passenger services was further delayed until 1 July as the Railway Inspector required alterations to one of the bridges. The Stroud extension was always worked separately from the main branch and passengers were required to make a change of trains at Dudbridge; a single-coach push-and-pull then worked the one and a quarter miles to Stroud Wallbridge. The journey took just four minutes and the shuttle soon became known as the 'Dudbridge Donkey'. In 1914, *The Railway and Travel Monthly* compared the Midland service to Stroud with that offered by the Great Western and concluded gloomily that it 'does not compare at all favourably'.

In the early years, there was the occasional flurry of interest in turning the Nailsworth branch into part of a longer through route but it is difficult to tell with what seriousness these schemes were proposed. At one stage, the Midland planned to create its own direct line to Salisbury via an upgraded Nailsworth branch and the fledgling Malmesbury Railway, but the scheme was dropped when the Midland and Great Western reached a territorial agreement. Then in 1882, a bill was introduced in Parliament for a Thames and Severn Railway from Stroud to Siddington near Cirencester. This would largely follow the course of the Thames and Severn Canal and was supported, *inter alia*, by the Severn and Wye Railway. This company was then suffering greatly from GWR competition and sought its own direct route to London and Southampton, but the bill failed and the scheme was never revived.

Locally, the impact of the Nailsworth railway was somewhat limited and not at all what the early promoters might have hoped, although economic factors had more to do with this than any intrinsic fault in the line itself. It certainly set the seal on Nailsworth's development as a place in its own right for, before the railway arrived, it was nothing more than a collection of hamlets which, officially at least, belonged to other local parishes such as Minchinhampton, Avening and Horsley. The railway also gave local people a greater degree of mobility, especially children who travelled regularly to schools at Ryeford and Dudbridge. However, Nailsworth and the valley leading to it had traditionally relied on the woollen industry which was in a steady decline throughout the nineteenth century. As early as 1821, William Cobbett wrote of a depression in the wool trade 'partly due to the introduction of machinery' and the sustained depression of 1873 to 1896 only made matters worse. Some of the mills switched to other activities, a notable example being the manufacture of walking sticks which was made possible by abundant supplies of cheap local beechwood. This was evidently a boon for generations of naughty little boys, for the off-cuts could be used to make pea-shooters. However, this was hardly the traffic on which railway fortunes could be built! A more significant local traffic was livestock to Nailsworth market and Irish pigs to Hillier's slaughterhouse, again in Nailsworth. William Malpas, a local resident, can remember driving these

The delightful rural setting of Nailsworth station on the former Midland Railway branch from Stonehouse. Passenger services on this line were suspended as early as 1947 although it was not officially closed to passengers until 1949, while freight continued to run until 1966
Lens of Sutton

animals from the station for a halfpenny a time. He recalls that unloading them was not a pleasant job, for they were shipped over via Liverpool and spent up to seven days in the same railway wagon; they arrived in Nailsworth with plenty of muck and bad odour! Then on the drive up to the slaughterhouse, they would 'get everywhere, especially in people's gardens'.

The train services were generally modest. When the main branch opened, three passenger trains were provided daily taking twenty to twenty-five minutes for the five and three-quarter miles. The line suffered from sharp curves and gradients, as a result of which the average speed was only 18 mph. On the freight side, a maximum of twenty wagons was also imposed. William Malpas can remember the later passenger service and recalls that the first train went out at 6 a.m. while the last one arrived back at 10 p.m. Visitors used to stay at The Railway Hotel while locals were met by pony and trap. He has vivid memories of the summer specials to Weston-super-Mare, when up to twelve coaches would be provided on the branch-line train. Passengers had to change at Stonehouse and faced a journey of Herculean proportions. They departed at six in the morning and could expect to reach Weston by one in the afternoon; they would then have three hours of sun and sand before starting their return journey, which finished at ten o'clock at night. He can recall 'tired kids crying with their buckets and spades' and the 'never no more' vows of their parents because they had misbehaved. Racing pigeons were also sent out by train to destinations such as Ashchurch, Bromsgrove and Tamworth. Over the years, the pigeon fanciers got more and more adventurous until one batch of birds was sent to Thurso; the winning pigeon covered the 580 miles in thirteen and a half hours.

With the 1923 grouping, the line passed into the hands of the London, Midland and Scottish Railway which, on 14 June 1947, withdrew passenger services as one of its last economies. This step was intended initially to be temporary but the newly-formed British Railways confirmed the withdrawal as permanent in 1949. Thereafter, the only passenger trains were specials chartered by the Gloucestershire Railway Society. Freight traffic lingered on for another seventeen years but was withdrawn on 1 June 1966. The last train was a diesel shunter with twelve trucks. The council leaflet on the railway walk records that, 'although the event passed without ceremony, there was one passenger with a camera, although no one knew who he was or where he came from'. Someone, somewhere may still have a valuable record of the last day of this little-known Gloucestershire railway.

The Line Today

After the line closed, it lay abandoned for some seventeen years, largely forgotten. The present trail was built by the Stroud Job Creation Group, supported by Stroud District Council, Gloucestershire County Council, the Countryside Commission and the Manpower Services Commission. Construction commenced in 1983 and the route was formally opened in 1985. After such a long period of neglect, the amount of undergrowth obstructing the line must have been formidable – small wonder that it took two years to put it back on its feet.

The permanent way is now owned by the county council and remains intact with the exception of a small section in the vicinity of Woodchester station, where the old formation has been used to re-align the nearby A46. Fortunately, a new link path of exceptionally high quality has been provided alongside the road to preserve the continuity of the route.

The original stations were at Ryeford, Dudbridge and Nailsworth, later additions being Woodchester (north of Nailsworth) and Stroud Wallbridge. Unless we count the empty platforms at Dudbridge, only Nailsworth survives: when Revd Mills blessed the site in 1864, he clearly had a far-reaching influence! As befitted the company's headquarters, Nailsworth was the grandest station on the line, an elegant structure built of Cotswold stone with fine decorative features in the classical style. Recently it was undergoing restoration as a private dwelling. Ryeford and Dudbridge were built in a similar style, so it makes it especially disappointing that they have been demolished. Woodchester and Stroud Wallbridge, alas, were cheap, utilitarian timber structures erected by the Midland Railway; miraculously, that at Stroud survived until 1986.

Walk 1 – Nailsworth to Stonehouse (5½ miles)

The walk starts in Nailsworth at grid reference 850998, just north of The George Hotel. Recently, this helpful landmark was threatened with demolition and the building was bedecked with protest notices; it remains to be seen whether or not it survives as a hotel. In the event that it is demolished, look out for the old Railway Hotel, which may be seen through the trees; the walk starts just opposite.

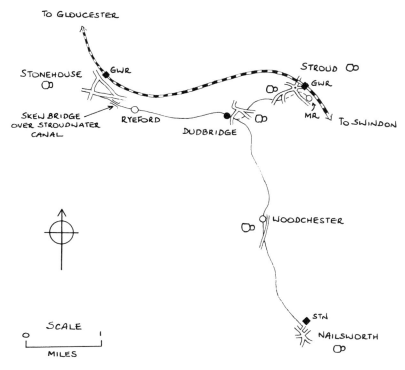

The Stroud Valleys Pedestrian Cycle Trail

The attractive Nailsworth station is now privately owned and does not, alas, form part of the walk. In the winter months, it may be glimpsed through the trees or, alternatively, can be viewed from the lane to Watledge and Minchin-hampton Common. This affords a splendid view of the station in a delightful woodland setting, which characterizes a large part of the walk. Unfortunately, a planning development has been submitted to Stroud District Council for the construction of seven dwellings on the site, so the station's seclusion may not last much longer.

The walk starts off past Egypt Mill (so called because one of its early owners was named Pharaoh Webb) and then enters a tunnel of trees; there are plenty of elderberries here for any walkers with an interest in home winemaking. The line then passes a succession of mills which emphasize the manufacturing history of the area. Dunkirk Mill (grid reference 845005) is particularly large; it was a wool mill until closure in 1891 and was later occupied by Walkers, gentlemen's outfitters. William Malpas referred to it as 'Walker's Stick Mill', so it must have produced walking sticks at some stage in its history as well. It has recently been restored as living accommodation. Opposite, there is a solitary hornbeam tree surrounded by saplings; the hornbeam is a type of beech tree with particularly tough wood which was used for making cog wheels in mills.

Woodchester station stood at grid reference 842023. The station house remains but little else, following a realignment of the A46 north of this point onto the old trackbed. This continues for just over a quarter of a mile but, as noted above, a new segregated path has been provided so that the continuity of the route is not broken. Woodchester is a delightful hotchpotch of rustic stone cottages on the west side of the valley; its roads are very narrow and incredibly steep. The village's chief claim to fame is a substantial Roman villa of more than sixty rooms which was discovered in the eighteenth century. The principal mosaic, known as the 'Woodchester pavement', portrays Orpheus charming the animals but the remains are kept buried except for occasional inspection by archaeologists.

Beyond Woodchester station, the line enters a cutting and passes under a bridge with an attractive cast-iron parapet (grid reference 842029); another bridge near Stonehouse is built to the same pattern. Both now require extra supports to cope with the weight of traffic passing over them. The bridge here carries the Selsley Road over the railway up onto the steep scarp of the Cotswolds; anyone who ventures this way is rewarded with magnificent views across the Vale of Berkeley and the River Severn. The approach to Dudbridge remains very sylvan, especially in summer, and, if photographed, would appear to be in the depths of the Gloucestershire countryside. In fact, the bird song is drowned out by the clanking of industrial machinery, but this is soon passed.

At Dudbridge, the line swings sharply west for the final two and a half miles into Stonehouse. Dudbridge, of course, was once the junction for Stroud where passengers changed trains to catch the 'Dudbridge Donkey'. The start of the old branch line can still be seen at grid reference 835044, curving away to the north-east. It is betrayed by a long curved wall built from blue engineering bricks which was presumably erected to shield residents of the nearby house from the unseemly sight and sound of the railway. To judge by its size and style, this property may once have belonged to a local mill-owner. The branch can be followed for a hundred yards or so but then abruptly stops in the path of a new housing estate built on the site of a former embankment; resisting the obvious, the developers have named this 'Dudbridge Meadows'.

Beyond the junction, the line passes under the B4066 and then reaches the site of Dudbridge station. The bridge carrying the B road was infilled after the line's closure and has only recently been pierced by a new pedestrian tunnel, which is rather like a huge corrugated-iron drain. While it would not win any prizes for aesthetics, it does well on the grounds of convenience by avoiding an irritating detour. Sadly, the station buildings have all been removed and even the platforms are half buried as a result of regrading the surface, but some railway atmosphere is provided by a large retaining wall on the west side which is again built from blue engineering brick. A large recess reveals where the passenger shelter once stood. At the west end of the station site, the magnificent Ebley Mill can be glimpsed through the trees. This is one of the largest mills in the area; it was designed in 1865 by G.F. Bodley, a leading industrial architect, and is arguably the finest industrial building for miles. It was used for wool production until the 1940s, since when its history has been rather patchy: parts remained in use for carding and spinning, while others were taken over by Daniel Greenaway, a printing firm. Locals report that it has now been restored and is in use by Stroud District Council but the restoration costs were a very contentious issue. Perhaps in time the furore will die down and be forgotten; at least the council has not constructed a modern eyesore.

The line now enters the valley of the River Frome and runs along its rural southern slopes. The scenery is in complete contrast to that on the earlier part of the walk, for the rambler is now offered expansive views across open country-side – a typical Gloucestershire landscape of steep rounded hills with thickly wooded clumps. On the left-hand side, a Midland Railway boundary marker is passed in an adjoining field; there may be others, buried in luxuriant summer foliage. A low bridge crosses the River Frome at grid reference 820044, the site of Ryeford station being met at grid reference 814045. No evidence of the station survives, the area having been turned over to light industrial use and a BMX track. Unfortunately for the council, youthful sporting fashions change very rapidly and the BMX track was totally unused on the occasion of my visit. A similar fate befell the one-time mania for skateboards!

The final feature of interest is in many ways the best, a long skew bridge over the Stroudwater Canal (grid reference 810047) though, as Anthony Burton rightly says, you need to get down on to the towpath to appreciate it. The canal crossing was the cause of considerable difficulty to the Stonehouse and

Skew bridge over the Stroudwater Canal west of Ryeford. This bridge, and the difficulties experienced in constructing it, exacerbated the poor financial state of the Stonehouse and Nailsworth Railway

Nailsworth Railway during the line's construction, and perhaps the directors would be pleased to see it giving good service over 120 years after it was built. At one time, the canal and railway met in mutual dereliction but both are now enjoying a revival. The Stroudwater, Thames and Severn Canal Trust hopes to restore the long-abandoned Thames–Severn canal link and has already carried out much repair work to the canal and associated structures. Walkers can therefore expect to see signs of restoration and clearance such as dredgers and silt barges. The line finally passes Stonehouse Upper Mill before joining the A419 by The Ship Inn. It is now just a third of a mile to the centre of the town. Walkers should proceed past The Ship and turn right into a local road which leads directly to the town post office, from where the Stroud buses depart.

Walk 2 – Dudbridge to Stroud (1 mile)

This is hardly a major railway walk, but Gloucestershire County Council deserves credit both for its thoroughness and for linking the main railway path

Cycle path on the former Midland Railway in Stroud. The lavish bridge carries the road from Stroud to Butterow; the Clothiers Arms stands at the top of the embankment on the left

with Stroud. Due to the new housing development mentioned above, the continuity of the branch is broken just to the east of Dudbridge station, but the council's route guide clearly shows 'negotiations pending for right of access'. Walkers must therefore leave the station by the old approach road and turn left on reaching the B4066. In a few hundred yards, this joins the A46 by a large garage; Kimmins Flour Mill is passed on the way, complete with a large water-wheel leaning against the south-facing wall. Turn right at the garage and then fork left by The Railway Inn, appropriately decorated in Midland Railway colours. Immediately after a bridge at grid reference 837046, a new access ramp has been constructed which gives access to the trackbed below.

The line was built on the south side of the river valley and, like the 'main' line to Nailsworth, has a distinctly rural look considering the developed area through which it passes. A substantial iron bridge carries a main road over the line at grid reference 843048, followed shortly by a most impressive brick bridge, constructed from the now familiar blue engineering bricks. From both of these it is obvious that the trackbed was made wide enough to accommodate double track; how optimistic those early railway builders were!

Shortly after the second bridge, the cycle path leaves the trackbed and swings left to join the main road down into Stroud. It alights opposite The Clothiers Arms, which is extremely convenient for anyone who has worked up a thirst.

The pub still sports a sign for the Stroud Brewery Company (long taken over and closed down) while the bar windows feature attractive stained-glass panels with the legend 'SBCo'. Modern brewery accountants must shudder at the thought of such extravagance. The old railway had a number of other engineering features before it reached its terminus but we are now close to Stroud town centre and much redevelopment has taken place. Despite this, a brick viaduct still remains just south of a large roundabout at grid reference 848051, its survival no doubt dictated by the small businesses which trade 'underneath the arches'. The site of the Midland Railway's Stroud station cannot be deduced exactly, but it was about 300 yds due south of the existing GWR station. Walkers should look for Wallbridge Upper Lock, which formed the end-on junction between the Stroudwater and Thames & Severn canals. This still survives, awaiting restoration, although the east end has been blocked off to conserve water in the higher level. A road bridge used to cross this lock from north to south. Today, only the northern abutment remains but, once again, it features the blue engineering bricks so common in Midland Railway construction. The road it once carried is called Wallbridge and I would guess that this was once the approach to Stroud's other station. The Bell Hotel stands at the north end of Wallbridge and this was probably once the station hotel. Those who despair of craftsmanship in the modern age should study this building carefully, for the extension was constructed in 1989 and matches the original in every detail.

Further Explorations

The Stroud Valleys Pedestrian Cycle Trail is just about it for railway walks in the area, but the local canals offer scope for those whose thirst for industrial archaeology is still not satisfied. The Stroudwater, Thames and Severn Canal Trust has published an excellent guide entitled *A Canal Walk Through Stroud*, copies of which can be obtained from the Tourist Information Office in Stroud High Street. This describes in great detail a canal walk of fourteen miles from Eastington near Stonehouse to Daneway near the western portal of the famous Sapperton Tunnel. This was the third longest canal tunnel constructed in this country and is 3,817 yds long – well over two miles. It was built ruler straight and a number of airshafts still punctuate the Bathurst estate beneath which it passes. The western part of the canal was built to accommodate wide-beamed Severn trows, but the eastern section was a standard narrow gauge canal with locks that were only 7 ft wide; railway enthusiasts may wonder if this had some subconscious impact on Brunel's choice of gauge. The two canal gauges met at Brimscombe, where goods had to be trans-shipped from wide- to narrow-beam vessels. Brimscombe's development as a substantial inland port was at the cost of speed and operating convenience on the canal itself. The last loaded boat travelled its entire length in 1911. The Thames and Severn was abandoned in stages in 1927 and 1933, the Stroudwater Canal holding on until about 1954. Surprisingly, it was only in the 1970s that most of the lock gates finally disintegrated although the modern walker will see evidence of restoration, particularly at the Eastington end and at the west end of Sapperton Tunnel.

A canal walk of an entirely different kind is offered by the Gloucester and Sharpness Canal which runs the sixteen miles between the two places named in its title. This is a ship canal which enables sea-going vessels to reach the port at Gloucester and, as such, it has never closed. A towpath follows the canal for fifteen miles, the exception being the docks area in Gloucester itself. Narrow-beamed pleasure craft can reach the canal via the River Avon and the northern reaches of the River Severn. The canal is fully staffed with crossing keepers who operate the swing bridges along its route and walkers will see the unusual spectacle of waterway traffic lights. Two locations of particular interest are the stretch immediately north of Sharpness Harbour (the sea locks here are gigantic) and Saul Junction, where the Stroudwater Canal crossed the Gloucester and Sharpness at right angles. Part of the Stroudwater is used for mooring pleasure craft but the western extension to the Severn peters out within a few feet where it enters an overgrown lock, choked with weeds. The gates at the west end would probably disintegrate if anyone attempted to move them.

The Sharpness area has been left till last deliberately for, half a mile north of the docks, the last remains of the Severn Bridge still stand. The sad history of the bridge is described in the previous chapter but not all of it could be sacrificed to the cutter's torch. The line from Sharpness approached the River Severn on a high embankment, culminating in a short but lofty stone viaduct which brought the line to the edge of the canal; this still stands. Trains then ran onto a swing bridge over the canal before passing the first pier of the bridge proper. The swing bridge, being metal, suffered the same fate as the main piers and spans but it rested on a circular stone bridge house which, like the viaduct, still survives. It is satisfying to know that something of this breathtaking structure remains if only to prove that the Severn Bridge was something more than an aberration in some railway history, so thoroughly has the rest of it been removed. The canal towpath is separated from the River Severn by a stone wall, beyond which a number of Severn barges lie moored up for ever, rusting away in terminal decay.

Transport and Facilities

Maps: Ordnance Survey: Landranger Series Sheet 162 (recommended)
Gloucestershire County Council: Stroud Valleys Pedestrian
  Cycle Trail Route Guide (recommended)

The county council leaflet is packed with information and an
absolute bargain at 20p, although readers should add a little extra
to cover return postage. Copies can be obtained from:

Gloucestershire County Council, Planning Department,
Countryside Section, Shire Hall, Gloucester, GL1 2TH

Buses: Stroud Valleys
Bus Station, Merrywalks, Stroud, Gloucestershire
Telephone: Stroud (045 36) 3421

Trains: British Rail Telephone Enquiry Bureau
Telephone: Gloucester (0452) 29501

A glance at the map will show that this is a well-populated area with tentacles of
development reaching out from Stroud into the surrounding valleys – the legacy
of prosperous days in the wool industry. Happily, the area still enjoys good bus
and train services so walkers will have little difficulty if they decide to use public
transport.

At the western end of the route, British Rail still has main-line stations at
Stroud and Stonehouse, served by an hourly train on the Swindon to Cheltenham line, although the Sunday service is rather patchy and would need
checking first. However, the service would be convenient for anyone who
wanted to walk from Ryeford to Stroud Wallbridge. The existing station at
Stroud is interesting inasmuch as it possesses one of the few surviving broad
gauge engine sheds by the station car park.

The local bus services are even more lavish in their provision. The main
routes are service 21 (Stroud to Stonehouse) and 34 (Stroud to Nailsworth).
During the daytime, these run every twenty minutes and every hour
respectively; a variety of other routes run from Stroud to Nailsworth, making a
service of two buses per hour. Evening and Sunday services are infrequent but
at least they still run. A third option would be to make a round walk, travelling
out by the old railway and back by the Stroudwater Canal towpath, which
follows the line all the way from Ryeford to Stroud Wallbridge.

On the refreshments side, there is no shortage of pubs and other establishments in Stonehouse, Stroud or Nailsworth. In fact, all along the line, the walker is never far from civilization – the wonder is that the railway has such a rural aspect. The usual monopoly of big brewers sits heavily upon the district but a number of enterprising free houses offer beers from more local companies such as Uley, Hook Norton and Wadworth. The Ram at Woodchester (grid reference 839021) and The Clothiers Arms at Stroud both offer a wide range of ales, and The Ram offers good food. It is interesting to note how both pub names reflect the industry on which the area's wealth was founded; other examples are not hard to come by, such as The Weavers Arms, The Fleece Inn and The Woolpack.

5
THE MIDLAND AND SOUTH WESTERN JUNCTION RAILWAY, WILTSHIRE

Swindon to Rushey Platt and Chiseldon to Marlborough

Introduction

For many people, the name Swindon conjures up visions of the Great Western Railway and the famous works which were once so important to the town. It may come as a surprise, therefore, to discover that a rival concern was once based here – the Midland and South Western Junction Railway. This ran from Cheltenham to Andover via Cirencester, Swindon and Marlborough and, at Andover, exercised running powers over the London and South Western Railway's Test Valley line to Romsey and Southampton. The MSWJR could thus promote itself as an independent main line which connected the Midlands with the Solent and Bournemouth areas. Its ambitions were most unwelcome to the GWR, which demonstrated its hostility frequently, not least in an unsuccessful legal action of 1881 which sought to prevent the upstart company bridging its Bristol main line west of Swindon.

The jealousy with which the Great Western guarded its territory is well known but, despite this, it suffered the indignity of three north to south 'invaders' – from west to east, the Somerset and Dorset, the Midland and South Western Junction and the Didcot, Newbury and Southampton Railways. The Somerset and Dorset was forced to sell out by the high cost of constructing its northern extension to Bath, but escaped into the hands of the LSWR and Midland Railway when the Great Western thought it had it securely in its grasp. The Didcot, Newbury and Southampton Railway was an over-ambitious company which got out of its depth financially and politically; it ended up a rather diminished affair, firmly in the grip of the GWR. Only the Midland and

THE MIDLAND AND SOUTH WESTERN JUNCTION RAILWAY, WILTSHIRE

Intended as a through route between the Midlands and the South Coast, the former MSWJR line had the melancholy distinction of being one of the first major line closures instigated by the Western Region in 1961. In this charming view of Ogbourne station its independent company origins are apparent with the unique MSWJR style of architecture and an ornate station lamp. The train is headed by a 'Duke' class engine heading north from Marlborough towards Swindon

Lens of Sutton

South Western Junction Railway achieved anything approaching genuine independence and this, like its modest prosperity, was very much due to the efforts of Sam Fay who put the company on its feet when financial ill-health and Great Western hostility had brought it to its knees.

The enthusiasm which individual railways attract and the extent to which they survive closure as recreational paths is largely, if not wholly, unpredictable. The MSWJR enjoys a good bibliography and more of its route can be walked today, officially and without obstruction, than either the Somerset and Dorset or the Didcot, Newbury and Southampton lines. In their way, these are fitting tributes to a plucky cross-country railway which carved out a place and purpose for itself in the face of very serious obstacles. One elderly passenger from Romsey recalled the old line with obvious affection; in its heyday, it was a 'byword for efficiency'. Trains still call at his local station but none travel to Cheltenham via the Midland and South Western; that now is just another part of the lost age of service and punctuality.

History

Plans for a railway from the industrial Midlands to the south coast were first promulgated in the 1840s, the heady days of the railway mania, but prompted fierce opposition from the Great Western Railway and came to nothing. When the idea was revived in the 1870s, it appealed mainly to towns such as Marlborough, Cricklade and Cirencester which were either poorly served by rail or not on the network at all.

In May 1872, James Copleston Townsend, a Swindon solicitor, promoted a scheme which would extend the GWR Savernake to Marlborough branch northwards to Swindon and southwards to Andover; the title adopted was the Swindon, Marlborough and Andover Railway. The GWR was initially sympathetic, with the result that the necessary parliamentary acts were passed with little difficulty in the summer of 1873. The first sod was turned at Marlborough on 28 July 1875 after which the serious work began at the Swindon end.

The railway's intention was to bore through Swindon Hill, an unfortunate choice of route as it turned out. The geology was particularly difficult and there were frequent landslips, with the result that tunnelling ground to a halt in October 1876 and the excavations were abandoned; they were subsequently infilled and Hunt Street built above them. The company now teetered on the brink of bankruptcy and was only kept alive by the enthusiasm of Townsend and one or two other local directors. In July 1878, they obtained an Act for a time extension and, a year later, an Act for deviations which allowed them to solve the Swindon Hill problem by skirting round its western slopes to Rushey Platt, where a junction could be formed with the GWR. This proved considerably easier than the tunnel scheme but there were still problems, particularly in the low-lying marshes around the Wilts and Berks Canal, which was still in use, although returning regular losses by this date. One thousand tons of stone had to be poured into the wetlands here to create a solid foundation for a high embankment and bridge.

South of Swindon, a substantial embankment was required to take the line into Chiseldon. This alone took nine months to build and required the movement of 20,000 cu yds of chalk and earth, most of it dug out manually, but construction was then much easier. Stations were provided at Chiseldon, Ogbourne St George and Marlborough, the line finally opening on 26 July 1881.

The GWR had seemed indifferent during construction but now became openly hostile. This is explained by the new railway's friendliness with the LSWR, at that time bent on aggression, and the consequent spectre of a rival north–south line marching right through the middle of traditional GWR territory. The Swindon–Marlborough section was now open to traffic and the southern extension to Andover was nearing completion. Through trains began running from Swindon to Andover on 5 February 1883 but, by then, the GWR had developed a stranglehold over the new railway by creating difficulties at Swindon and over its existing Marlborough branch, which formed an integral part of the new route.

The Swindon, Marlborough and Andover Railway was already financially weak due to its high capital expenditure and was soon disappointed with the low level of passenger receipts over its line. The GWR then reduced its freight rates in order to squeeze out the intruder; this forced the SMAR into the realization that it had to forge north to link up with the Midland Railway at Cheltenham if it was to stand any chance of success. The result was the Swindon and Cheltenham Extension Railway, which aimed to construct a line from Rushey Platt to Cricklade, Cirencester and Andoversford, where it would join the Banbury and Cheltenham Direct Railway. Work commenced in spring 1882 and services to Cirencester started on 18 December 1883. In June 1884, no doubt anticipating completion, the SMAR and SCER amalgamated to form the Midland and South Western Junction Railway but, alas, the Cheltenham extension was another precarious financial venture. A receiver was appointed on 20 December 1884 on a petition from the company's own engineer, who was owed £5,663 – a very considerable sum in those days. In a very bold move, the creditors and stockholders decided not to wind the company up but to raise the extra capital needed to reach Cheltenham. As a result, work recommenced in 1888 and through services began running to Cheltenham on 1 August 1891.

Unfortunately, the line was now very run down and dilapidated: fences were broken, locomotives and rolling stock in a sorry state and the time-keeping of the company's trains quite appalling. In late 1891, the MSWJR therefore approached the LSWR for advice on how to run its railway more efficiently. The LSWR responded with a most remarkable and unselfish gesture – it transferred Sam Fay, one of its best railwaymen, to the company for a period of seven years. Fay took charge on 1 February 1892 and immediately embarked on a policy of promotion, improvement and reform. He obtained cheaper coal supplies, increased advertising revenue and set up a fund for much needed new locomotives and rolling stock. Then in November 1892, he secured agreement with the LSWR for running powers over the Test Valley line from Andover to Southampton; this paved the way for a regular Southampton to Cheltenham express and, by 1894, popular excursions were reaching destinations such as Bournemouth. So successful were these policies that the MSWJR was able to settle with its creditors in November 1897, thus securing release from the hands of the receiver. However, most importantly of all, Fay recognized that the key to securing the company's future lay in removing the GWR Marlborough branch from its route. With this in mind, he created a new company which constructed an independent line from Marlborough to Savernake. The first trains ran on 26 June 1898 and, on that date, the junctions with the GWR were taken out of use. The MSWJR could now regard itself as truly independent.

The Midland and South Western Junction Station, Marlborough.

This railway forms communication towards the south with Southampton and the Isle of Wight, and on the north joins the Midland Railway at Cheltenham.

The MSWJR station at Marlborough; the GWR terminus was to the rear of the houses in the background. This was one of the more important stations on the line from Cheltenham to Andover and saw much traffic from the famous school at the start and end of each term

Lens of Sutton

While it never made its investors a fortune, the line certainly ran well and justified its existence. Although initially laid as single track, all of the route bar the section from Marlborough to Cirencester was doubled. Services reached a peak in 1913 but never recovered after the First World War. The first serious blow came as early as 1 July 1923, when the company was absorbed by the GWR. This was a logical step inasmuch as the MSWJR was deeply embedded in GWR territory but it made its line the helpless victim of GWR animosity; some MSWJR employees actually moved away to join the Southern rather than work for the old enemy. While the GWR made good the wear and tear of the war years, it singled the Cheltenham extension and ran down services so that the line became a sluggish rural backwater. The Second World War brought a flood of military traffic which greatly revived its fortunes and, during the build-up to D-Day, it was kept open twenty-four hours a day. However, the revival was shortlived and most of the wartime improvements were removed in 1950. Thereafter, the decline continued. On 30 June 1958, through services between Cheltenham and Andover were reduced to one each way; then on 9 September 1961, passenger services were withdrawn completely. There is an interesting footnote to closure inasmuch as British Railways was then not geared for the wholesale butchery of lines which followed; thus the timetable for 1961/62 accidentally included two pages of services from Andover to Cheltenham which never ran. It would be interesting to know how many intending travellers were deceived by this unintentional piece of publicity for the line.

Various sections were retained for freight working but these gradually died away and, by the end of the 1970s, only Andover to Ludgershall and Swindon Town to Moredon remained, together with the link to the GWR at Rushey Platt. Ludgershall was kept open for military traffic, Swindon Town for oil traffic and Moredon for the occasional train to the power station. By the early 1980s, the oil traffic had dried up and Moredon power station, like the MSWJR, was also declared redundant. Today, only the spur from Andover to Ludgershall remains, reflecting the days when the military branch from Ludgershall to Tidworth was the biggest revenue-earner on the whole line. The demise of the Midland and South Western Junction Railway can be traced back to 1923, when it passed into the hands of the GWR. The line depended for its survival on committed promotion and management. As the exodus of some employees revealed, many then doubted the GWR's ability to provide these qualities and history appears to have proved them right.

The Line Today

After closure, a considerable proportion of the line was acquired by Wiltshire County Council. Part of it now lies beneath the M4, which makes its noisy way around the south of Swindon, and a similar fate was planned for the section from Chiseldon to Ogbourne St George as part of a 'long term road project'. In the short term, much of the trackbed from Chiseldon to Marlborough was let out on one-year renewable leases. Many adjoining landowners and householders thus acquired short lengths for garden extensions and pony grazing, although one or two used the line unofficially and, strictly speaking, had no right to be there. This is a common problem with redundant land of any description but creates difficulties for railway ramblers and cycle path builders alike, particularly if the trackbed has been used for dumping, of which there was some evidence on the occasion of my visit.

In this part of Wiltshire at least a solution is at hand, for in 1988 Sustrans Ltd took out a twenty-five year lease on the trackbed from Chiseldon to Marlborough with the express intention of converting it into a cycleway. The company's plans were to clear the route for use as a footpath by the end of 1988 and to construct a cycleway along it by the end of 1989. Unfortunately, the project was delayed by the closure of the Community Programme which customarily provided the labour for such schemes, but the company had made a start by early 1989 and, with the assistance of International Volunteer Services, planned a summer work camp to complete the path surfacing.

In the event, the main work was done by two IVS work camps, each lasting three weeks and comprising twenty people from all over Europe, plus a great deal of weekend voluntary work. In September 1989 Sustrans announced that the path was complete as far as Ogbourne Maizey and the finished section was rapidly becoming popular with local people.

The section from Swindon Town station to Rushey Platt was converted somewhat earlier in 1986. Sustrans is managing this work as the 'Swindon, Marlborough and Great Bedwyn Project', which suggests that it intends to connect and extend its Swindon and Chiseldon paths despite the apparently formidable obstacle of the M4! Thus, after a long period of neglect and indifference, it looks as if the potential of the old line will finally be realized in the interests of recreation and road safety.

Walk 1 – Swindon Town to Rushey Platt (1½ miles)

This railway path starts in Station Approach, off Newport Street; walkers should look out for the Wheatsheaf public house which stands close by the junction of the two roads. Swindon Town station was actually located in Old Town and was occasionally known by that name; Swindon New Town is located about half a mile to the north near the GWR station and works, to which it owes its existence. The walker should continue to the end of Station Approach and there proceed down a flight of steps on the right. At the bottom, turn right again and look out for a wall mural which depicts Swindon Town's railway history. This features various characters involved in the history of the line, including Tim Binks (one of the Sustrans construction team) who can be seen levelling the cycle path with a mechanical roller. Though it is hard to believe, this is the site of Swindon Town station; a new trading estate now stands here, obliterating all recollection of the past.

The walk starts off by leading through a short tunnel just west of the old station site. It then opens out, giving good views of the hills to the south of Swindon. Most of the route is on an embankment flanked by large colonies of rosebay willowherb, which add a splash of deep pink during the summer months. The old Wilts and Berks Canal is crossed at grid reference 137834, the course still clearly discernible despite its abandonment in 1914. As described in the history section, the marshes surrounding the canal were the cause of considerable difficulty during construction. The site of Rushey Platt station is

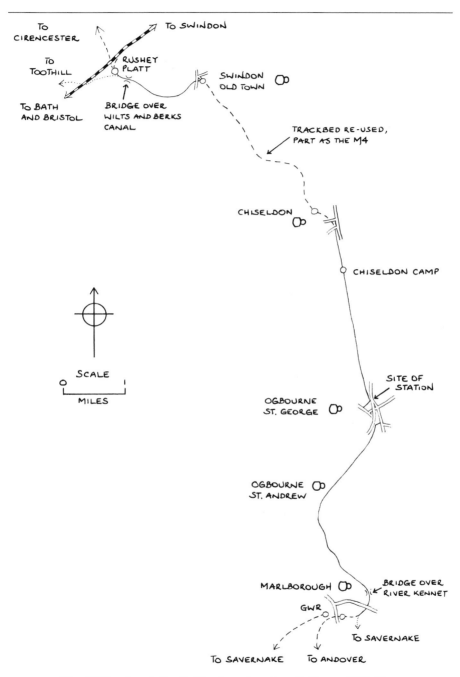

To CIRENCESTER

To SWINDON

To TOOTHILL

RUSHEY PLATT

SWINDON OLD TOWN

To BATH AND BRISTOL

BRIDGE OVER WILTS AND BERKS CANAL

TRACKBED RE-USED, PART AS THE M4

CHISELDON

CHISELDON CAMP

SCALE

MILES

SITE OF STATION

OGBOURNE ST. GEORGE

OGBOURNE ST. ANDREW

MARLBOROUGH

BRIDGE OVER RIVER KENNET

GWR

To SAVERNAKE

To SAVERNAKE

To ANDOVER

The Midland and South Western Junction Railway, Wiltshire

met at grid reference 133838. This once possessed a signal-box and four platforms, as it was situated on an important junction; the MSWJR main line continued north-west towards Cirencester and Cheltenham, while a branch swung away to the north-east to join the GWR main line for the one and a quarter mile run into the other Swindon station. However, the railway developers greatly overestimated Rushey Platt's importance and traffic potential with the result that it closed on 1 October 1905, unable to generate the revenue which would justify repairs and improvements. Today, only a few mounds of rubble remain.

The cycle path now dips away to the left and under the BR main line to reach Toothill, an area of new development which has sprung up since the line's closure. The old MSWJR stops at a fence, beyond which there is a steep climb to the former bridge over the GWR main line, now removed. This section is obviously private and probably still belongs to British Rail.

Walk 2 – Chiseldon to Marlborough (7½ miles)

Although this walk starts to the south of the main village, there is a convenient public car park at Chiseldon opposite the Elm Tree public house (grid reference 187798); few motorists who park here nowadays can realize that they are leaving their vehicles on the site of the former Chiseldon station. The Swindon–Marlborough bus service also stops nearby, which is handy for walkers using public transport. The railway path proper starts south of this location at grid reference 193794, the intervening cutting having been filled in and built on. One wonders how many of these homeowners realize that their dwellings are poised in 'mid-air' above the old permanent way! At the time of my visit, the trackbed had just been acquired by Sustrans Ltd and awaited conversion into a cycle path; walkers using this book can therefore expect to find a good number of changes and improvements.

The path starts as a narrow but easily followed trail which leads away to the south through an avenue of willow trees. Unfortunately, youngsters on motor cycles used to frequent the old railway here but the Sustrans conversion work now prevents them from gaining access. Chiseldon Camp Halt is reached at grid reference 195781. This was not one of the original stations but developed in response to the needs of the nearby military camp on the Downs. A siding to the camp was installed in September 1914, the halt proper being opened by the GWR on 1 December 1930 in a bid to counteract road competition. The halt today is an eerie place and it is difficult to deduce the original arrangement of

The girder bridge over Little Petherick Creek, Padstow

Horringford station is situated at the west end of a railway path from Sandown. Its delightful setting makes it a perfect example of a country railway station

things. A pair of gate posts survives and these may once have given access to the station yard. The site is also littered with very large overturned brick and mortar blocks, which were possibly anti-tank traps installed during the last war. Away to the west, no trace remains of the camp; only corn grows here now, although the old access roads still march purposefully across the fields.

South of Chiseldon Camp, the line was blocked by the earthworks of what appeared to be a gypsy encampment (grid reference 196777). In order to negotiate this obstruction, Sustrans purchased an acre of land to the east of the encampment which would accommodate a continuous path leading on through a prominent clump of pines. Immediately to the south, the line was terribly overgrown and the entire width of the formation blocked by a very dense growth of blackberries, hogweed and sapling trees. Sustrans worked on this throughout August 1989 to clear a way through – a sure indication of how bad things were. On the occasion of my trail-blazing visit, I was forced to follow the nearby A345 to the site of the next underbridge at grid reference 198766, where I regained the trackbed with some difficulty. In the wet summer of 1988, it was very difficult to conceive that any man-made thing had ever passed this way but, happily, a high quality all-weather path now exists here and ramps have been built at all the missing bridges.

A bungalow occupies the line at grid reference 198760; this is attached to a dog kennels and the owners made their objections to the cycle path quite clear. Fortunately, there is plenty of room at this location and the line runs on a slight embankment; the path therefore keeps to the foot of this to accommodate all interests, not least the residents' need for privacy. On the other hand, it does nothing but good to get cyclists off the busy A345, while both cyclists and walkers will enjoy the beautiful lineside views of wind-rippled cornfields and distant hills.

Beyond the dog kennels, the path disappears into trees and then a cutting, at the end of which stood Ogbourne St George station (grid reference 202744). This has been demolished, its remains buried beneath road improvement works. The A345 now occupies the course of the old line but the path swings right and runs down a track to a T-junction where the walker should turn left. In just over 200 yds, turn left again, proceed under the new road bridge and immediately turn right into a lane which leads up onto the Downs; the die-like straightness of this reveals that it was once a Roman road. The trackbed can be regained in a few hundred yards on the right.

Between Chiseldon and Ogbourne St George, the line crosses a generally flat plain with expansive views and, on a bad day, uninterrupted winds. Travellers on the Marlborough to Swindon horse-drawn bus complained bitterly of these in the days before the railway was built. Nowadays, the busy A345 is close at hand but an abundance of trees and hedges fortunately offer some screening from both the sight and sound of it. From Ogbourne St George to Marlborough, however, the character of the line changes dramatically as it begins its long approach to Marlborough along the valley of the River Og. The surrounding countryside makes it appear that the line is climbing steadily but the gradient profiles demonstrate that it actually approaches Marlborough on a ruling downhill gradient. I found this section easier to follow in that the undergrowth offered no obstructions which were entirely impassable, so Sustrans did not have too much difficulty in clearing the way for its cycle path. Most of the leases had already run out or were due to expire shortly, none of them being renewed due to the forthcoming re-use of the route. Most noticeably of all, the majority of man-made barriers along the line had already been removed; this created a very strong and satisfying impression that something was about to rise from the ashes of the past.

The ballast was still *in situ* on this section and, in places, patterns in the grass revealed where the sleepers once lay despite the line having closed as long ago as 1961. At grid reference 201732, a platelayer's hut has survived, a modern building probably dating from the D-Day preparations of 1943 onwards, like similar structures on the Didcot, Newbury and Southampton Railway. At Ogbourne St Andrew, garden extensions occupied the line but the Sustrans 'Schedule of Access Works' clearly showed the path going through; presumably these too were on renewable leases. Just south of the village, the trackbed was festooned with an abundance of wild strawberries which were very large and plump given the diminutive size of the species.

For the last two miles into Marlborough, the line runs on a succession of cuttings and embankments – a good example of the 'cut and fill' technique of construction. Cuttings were dug out and the spoil used to construct an embankment across the succeeding valley. Several graceful curved overbridges can be glimpsed through the overhanging foliage; they are easily missed, but perhaps clearance work will make them more visible in the future. Many of the residents adjoining the line in this area were concerned at the impact of the path on local wildlife; hopefully they were pleased that the conversion work proceeded under the direction of an ecologist. Sustrans has found from its experience with similar paths elsewhere in the country that they are generally regarded as creating very real benefits in terms of amenity and access to the countryside, while it must be remembered that a cycleway is a small intrusion compared with a new road, the fate originally intended for the northern part of the line at least.

The wooded seclusion of the path is interrupted briefly at grid reference 202692, where the old railway suddenly arrives at a bridge over the River Kennet. This is a very surprising encounter, to say the least, for the sheer height of the railway embankment is suddenly revealed. The walker should note especially the gigantic retaining walls which are beautifully finished in stone facing blocks. It is now barely a quarter of a mile to the A4 in Marlborough, where the road-over-rail bridge is a sorry sight, being shored up with great timber supports which were showing distinct signs of decay on the occasion of my visit. It is interesting to think that only railway ramblers are privy to this knowledge, the vast majority of motorists rushing overhead being oblivious to the precarious-looking structure which supports them; hopefully, the surveyor from the county Highways Department will pass this way before things become much worse. The path will leave the trackbed in another quarter of a mile at grid reference 199686, there turning south towards Postern Hill and Savernake Forest. Those wishing to stop at Marlborough can leave either here or at the A4, the latter giving quicker but noisier access to the town. Marlborough Low Level 'station used to stand at grid reference 194687. It is now used as a Highways Department depot but the station building has long been demolished: all that remains is a decaying buffer stop and a short length of platform, upon which the station's cattle pens once stood. However, this land is private and will not form part of the cycleway.

Further Explorations

As mentioned earlier, more of the MSWJR can be walked officially than either the Somerset and Dorset or the Didcot, Newbury and Southampton railways. Between Withington (grid reference 032159) and Chedworth (056113), the trackbed has been acquired by the Gloucestershire Trust for Nature Conservation and a very fine walk it makes too. Between Cirencester and Cricklade, Gloucestershire and Wiltshire county councils plan to convert the trackbed into a footpath passing through the Cotswold Water Park. From Cricklade towards Rushey Platt, Thamesdown Borough Council has acquired much of the line; its plans are not known but the Swindon and Cricklade Railway leases the section from Cricklade to Moredon and is actively relaying the line. Recently volunteers were busy constructing a new bridge over the River Ray, which extends the railway's scope considerably.

South of Marlborough, the trackbed is in private ownership. At present, there is no more official walking until south of Andover on the LSWR's Test Valley line, over which the MSWJR exercised running powers. This is now a public bridleway from Fullerton Junction (grid reference 381394) to just north of Mottisfont (334267), a delightful village largely owned by the National Trust. It is remarkable that so much of the route can be walked officially and it is tempting to wonder if the separate parts could somehow be linked together. This, alas, is probably just another impractical railway rambler's dream!

If any enthusiast of the MSWJR can forgive the GWR for its hostility, the fine Great Western Railway Museum in Swindon is definitely worth a visit. Apart from the larger exhibits, the museum contains a number of smaller items which reveal the atmosphere and importance of the railway in nineteenth-century

Reading Street in Swindon Railway Village. The village was constructed by the Great Western Railway to house its employees and was restored by Thamesmead Borough Council between 1966 and 1981. Even the drain covers bear the initials GWR

England. A case in point is an heraldic board from Newport, Gwent, on which the town's station-masters are listed like the past vicars of a church. The museum is surrounded by Swindon Railway Village, which Thamesdown Borough Council purchased from British Rail in 1966; restoration took the best part of fifteen years. The village accommodated workers from the nearby Great Western Railway Works and, in its day, was an example of very enlightened employer practice. The houses were of a very advanced design for the period, each property having a small front garden, its own privy and a wash house. The extent to which 'the company' dominated life in the community can be measured by the fact that even the drain covers were cast by the GWR foundry.

Close by, a potent reminder of modern times stands in advancing decay. The GWR Mechanics' Institution was founded in 1855; its premises still stand in Emlyn Square but Swindon has lost its need for mechanics, as witnessed by the recent closure of the railway works. The old institution looks ever more down at heel: many roof tiles are missing and the weather must wreak havoc inside. Time is dealing out blows to the Great Western Railway as well as its one-time enemies.

Transport and Facilities

Maps: Ordnance Survey: Landranger Series Sheets 173 and 174
Ordnance Survey: One-Inch Map Sheet 157 (recommended)

Most of this route appears on Landranger Sheet 173 with the exception of two long curves at Ogbourne St George and Marlborough which, inconveniently, just appear on Sheet 174. However, the discontinued one-inch Sheet 157 shows the line in its entirety; copies can usually be obtained from the address in Appendix A.

Buses: Swindon and District
Bus Station, Fleming Way, Swindon, Wiltshire
Telephone: Swindon (0793) 22243

Trains: British Rail Telephone Enquiry Bureau
Telephone: Swindon (0793) 36804

The section from Swindon Town station to Rushey Platt is short enough to be walked in both directions, so no apologies are made for omitting details of local bus services. For that matter, there is no shortage of pubs and cafés at the north end of Station Approach so refreshments are no problem either.

As for the main walk from Chiseldon to Marlborough, Swindon and District's service 70 is ideal. This runs every hour (Mondays to Saturdays) from Swindon to Marlborough, with the last bus leaving Marlborough shortly after 8 p.m. For most of the way, its route is never more than a quarter of a mile from the old line; only on the long horseshoe curve into Marlborough does this stretch to a full mile. Refreshments too are not a problem. There are pubs everywhere one would hope: at Chiseldon, Ogbourne St George, Ogbourne St Andrew and Marlborough, the last-named also possessing a number of good tea rooms. If only all railway walks could be provided with such convenient, civilized and abundant facilities!

6
THE CAMEL TRAIL

Padstow to Bodmin

Introduction

Bodmin Parkway station is some three and a half miles from the town it is intended to serve; the name makes it quite clear that passengers are expected to drive there. Despite this, Bodmin Parkway is probably a less forbidding name than the earlier Bodmin Road, with its connotation of being dropped miles from anywhere on a road which happens, eventually, to pass through Bodmin. All this helps to explain why Truro is now Cornwall's county town! When the railway revolution came to the duchy, Truro was placed on the important main line from Plymouth to Penzance while Bodmin was left to languish at the end of circuitous branch lines owned by rival companies. The fact that it boasted two stations was no substitute for that all important main-line connection.

In its time, Bodmin Road was the junction for a local service to Bodmin General, Wadebridge and Padstow. This was axed in 1967 but freight traffic survived for another sixteen years, serving Wadebridge until 1978 and Wenfordbridge (north of Bodmin) until 1983. Wenfordbridge used to provide a valuable traffic in china clay and, for many years, china clay wagons were occasionally stored in sidings to the north-west of the station site.

When the local trains to Padstow were withdrawn, Western National provided a replacement bus service and a single-decker of venerable age could sometimes be seen waiting under the trees on the station forecourt. A modern Leyland National vehicle now handles this traffic but, for most of the year, there is not much of it; hardly surprising in view of the diminished facilities and services. Even the station building is a disappointment, being a cheap flat-roofed affair of modern construction. It does not take long for a structure like this to look tatty.

But not all is doom and gloom. The Bodmin and Wenford Railway Company is now established at Bodmin General and has purchased the three and a half miles of track to Bodmin Parkway. With a combination of volunteer and paid labour, it has repaired this to a high standard. The long awaited visit of the

Railway Inspector took place on 30 September 1988 and the company's Light Railway Order was finally granted on 31 August 1989. As a result, a branch-line train may yet again depart from Bodmin Road's empty north platform.

History

The history of railways in the Bodmin area has as its central theme the history of the little Bodmin and Wadebridge Railway, a pioneering company which was running trains a full two years before the first public line in London. If this sounds surprising, it should be remembered that nineteenth-century Cornwall was a partly industrial mining county and, as such, was a fertile ground for invention and entrepreneurial skills. Some of the earliest names in the development of the steam engine are of Cornishmen such as William Murdock and Richard Trevithick.

As far as Bodmin was concerned, the attraction in the west was the River Camel which was navigable as far as Wadebridge. As early as 1797, an Act of Parliament was passed for a canal from Wadebridge to Dunmere but it was not pursued and the scheme lapsed. However, the interest in a westward connection remained and an Act for the Bodmin and Wadebridge Railway received the Royal Assent on 23 May 1832, the year of Lord John Russell's great Reform Act.

The young company unusually and fortuitously selected the standard gauge of 4 ft 8½ in; previous horse-drawn railways in the area had used 4 ft and 4 ft 6 in. On 1 February 1833, tenders were invited for rails and materials and, later that year, the line was being laid with 42 lb rails and granite block sleepers. This reveals that the line was intended to be worked by horses, as was the nearby Liskeard and Caradon Railway, but then a second instance of good fortune and inspiration occurred. In May 1833, a Mr Gurney offered to supply the railway with two steam engines and tenders, which he would keep in good order for six months after the start of services. Wisely, the company accepted. An order was placed in September that year: the locomotive was subsequently delivered in parts, assembled in Wadebridge and named *Camel* after the local river. It is interesting to note that *Camel* gave persistent trouble until October 1835, when it was discovered that her wheels were of different sizes; she had evidently been shaking herself to pieces.

The railway opened from Wadebridge to Bodmin on 4 July 1834, with branches to Ruthern Bridge and Wenfordbridge following on 6 August and 30 September respectively; these last two remained freight-only throughout their existence. The company very soon began to produce a healthy profit, with lime-rich sand (a simple but effective manure) going up the line towards

Bodmin and mineral traffic from a variety of mines coming back down. This happy state of affairs was to last for less than ten years for, by 1844, most of the mines were exhausted and competition had undermined the lucrative sand traffic. Things reached the point where half-yearly losses of 1200 were being recorded and then the company's staff had to endure substantial pay reductions.

Until this time, the Bodmin and Wadebridge had been entirely detached from the rest of the railway network but, as a matter of expediency, the directors now considered it necessary to link up with any other company which might propose a line in the area. There was no shortage of contenders but all fell through for one reason or another. One of these had been backed by the mighty London and South Western Railway and, when its scheme failed, it proceeded in 1846 to buy the Bodmin and Wadebridge regardless. Its intention was to keep the broad gauge out of north Cornwall but, acting without parliamentary sanction, its ownership of the line was to remain illegal until 1886, a fact exploited by the Great Western Railway to the full. Be that as it may, the LSWR did at least have a better balance sheet than the local company and provided some second-hand locomotives and rolling stock to keep it going. The Bodmin and Wadebridge thus struggled on until 1862, when it agreed to transport china clay on the line; this traffic later became its lifeblood.

By the late 1870s, competition between the LSWR and the GWR had developed to the point where each was backing alternate schemes which would incorporate the Bodmin and Wadebridge in the rest of the Cornish railway network. In 1880, the GWR obtained powers for an ambitious route from Delabole to Fowey via Wenford, Grogley and Ruthern Bridge; the commercial motivation for this was transporting Delabole slate to port. The LSWR retaliated in 1882 by backing the North Cornwall Railway's proposal for a line from Launceston to Wadebridge and Padstow, an Act for this reaching the statute book on 18 August of that year. An agreement was not reached until 1886, when the LSWR was allowed to legalize its ownership of the Bodmin and Wadebridge in return for upgrading the line to accommodate GWR trains as far as Wadebridge. This was very much a tactical victory for the GWR.

As a result of this, the LSWR became legal owner of the Bodmin and Wadebridge on 1 July 1886 and the GWR constructed a branch line to tap into it with remarkable speed. The section from Bodmin Road to Bodmin General opened on 27 May 1887, followed by an extension from Bodmin General to Boscarne on 3 September 1888. The Bodmin and Wadebridge was thus connected to the rest of the railway world, but to a main line owned and operated by its owner's deadly rivals.

Progress on the LSWR-backed North Cornwall Railway was very slow due to what Lewis Reade describes as a combination of 'bad luck, bad weather, difficult geology and recurring financial crises'. Thirteen years after the Act authorizing the line, the final section from Delabole to Wadebridge opened in

Terminus of the LSWR line at Padstow in Cornwall – the furthest west reached by the company's passenger lines from Waterloo. Traffic here was seasonal: the winter months saw little trade, while in the summer the trains had standing room only

Lens of Sutton

mid-1895. It was to be another four years before Padstow received its first train, the inaugural service running on 27 March 1899.

The network of lines around Bodmin was now complete and settled down to a steady existence of sixty-seven years. On 2 July 1906, halts were opened at Grogley, Nanstallon and Dunmere, the one at Grogley being unusual in that, during its early years, it was unlit and served only during daylight hours. The sand traffic which had so helped the early Bodmin and Wadebridge Railway petered out in the 1920s while the Ruthern Bridge branch closed on 30 December 1933, a victim of worked-out local mines and ever dwindling agricultural traffic. However, business on the other lines was still sound when the Bodmin and Wadebridge celebrated its centenary in September 1934.

With the advent of the Second World War, contingency plans were laid for diverting important Cornish trains if the need arose: GWR services were to travel via Launceston and Wadebridge, and Southern Railway services via Plymouth and Bodmin Road. The line from Boscarne to Wadebridge was upgraded as a precaution. These plans were put into action twice, in April and May 1941, when GWR trains had to avoid Plymouth on account of persistent heavy bombing by the Luftwaffe. This meant that Wadebridge and Boscarne

Beattie-designed 'Well Tank' No. 3314 on the delightfully scenic Wenfordbridge line, May 1938. Discussions are currently under way for returning a locomotive of this class to the present-day Bodmin and Wenford Railway

B.W. Anwell

played host to the prestigious 'Cornish Riviera Express', although the station foreman at Wadebridge must have welcomed the end of it: for the duration of the special arrangements he was working seventeen hours a day. The resultant journey must also have taxed the patience of all but the most devoted enthusiast, for four separate reversals were required – at Exeter St Davids, Wadebridge, Bodmin General and Bodmin Road.

With nationalization, all but the Bodmin General lines passed into the stewardship of the Southern Region of British Railways. They were transferred to the Western Region in 1950, back to the Southern in 1958 and then back to the Western in 1963. This last change inaugurated a rapid run-down of services and facilities. While this must have been inspired in large measure by the policies of Dr Beeching, it is difficult to avoid the conclusion that old inter-company rivalries played a part. The Western Region, as spiritual successor to the old Great Western Railway, was hardly going to butcher its own lines if cuts had to be made.

The North Cornwall line was the first to go and closed on 3 October 1966: fifty-seven miles of railway from Wadebridge to Okehampton were shut down at a stroke. A local service survived but not for long: the last train from Padstow to Bodmin Road ran on 30 January 1967 and a local shuttle from Boscarne to Bodmin North vanished with it for good measure.

The freight facilities in the area were greatly reduced but took a lot longer to kill off. Trains continued to run from Bodmin Road to Wadebridge for full wagon traffic until early in 1978. On 6 May that year, two final passenger trains ran from Plymouth to Wadebridge and back carrying 'Camel Train' headboards; the weather was appropriately dismal. The china clay traffic from Wenfordbridge survived until September 1983 but then it too was withdrawn and transferred to road. Those Cornish men and women who are unlucky enough to have their peace disturbed by modern juggernauts must regret decisions like this every day of the week.

The Line Today

Most of the Bodmin lines today are in local authority ownership. Cornwall County Council acquired the trackbed from Padstow to Wadebridge first and converted it into a railway path in 1980. With British Rail's abandonment of the line from Boscarne to Wadebridge, they then acquired this section and prepared plans for a 'Camel Trail' which would run all the way from Padstow to Bodmin, connecting at Dunmere with the old line to Bodmin North which is now owned by North Cornwall District Council.

Since British Rail abandoned the Wenfordbridge line in September 1983, the track from Bodmin Parkway to Bodmin General and Boscarne has been purchased by the Bodmin and Wenford Railway Company. This should ensure that the GWR route opened in 1887 and 1888 remains in use as a railway. The rest of the trackbed to Wenford has been taken over by North Cornwall District Council and will soon form an extension to the Camel Trail. The route can already be walked officially and gated access points have been provided, although the surface is very much as the railway left it. The district council applied for funds to carry out improvements in late 1988 and expected work to commence 'in the near future'.

The Walk (12½ miles)

Unlike some others, the start of this walk is blissfully easily to get to, being located at Padstow's old railway station. This is just south of the South Quay car park and also happens to be the terminus of the number 55 bus from Bodmin Parkway. If only all railway walks could be so conveniently arranged!

The station building is still in use and acts, among other things, as the

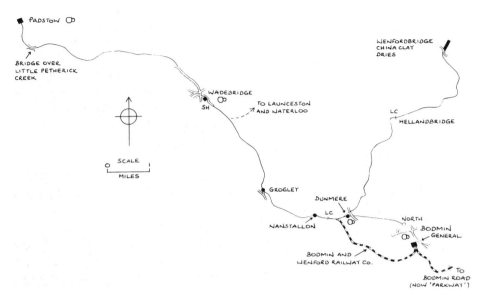

The Camel Trail

chamber for the local town council. It is of a standard design found all the way from here to Egloskerry, the last station before Launceston. Miraculously, all of these stations survive, none more completely than that at Camelford. Padstow also had a canopy, lamp room and signal-box but these have long been demolished. Reg Ridd was the last signalman at Padstow and, when the line closed, purchased the signal-box from British Rail. It arrived at his home in kit form: five lorry loads of stone, seventeen lengths of rail, a mound of roofing slates and eight large window frames which he has now incorporated into a summer-house in his garden. Like many old railwaymen, Reg remembers the railway being busy to the end and believes that men in high places made up their minds to close it. While heavy lorries had done serious damage to the line's freight traffic, the passenger trains still had a good holiday trade and regularly carried loads of schoolchildren for Wadebridge and Bodmin. The staff believed that they could have made it viable but were not given the chance.

On leaving the station, the walker should continue due south through a new car park and past the headquarters of the local sea scouts: the official start of the path will be found at grid reference 922749. This leads into a deep cutting hewn out of rock at the foot of Dennis Hill, before reaching the main engineering feature of the line, a three-span girder bridge over Little Petherick Creek. This was built in 1898 and was recently redecked by the county council. At low tide, it is possible to gaze over the edge into pools which form around the base of the

An imposing view of the triple-span girder bridge over Little Petherick Creek just east of Padstow. This is a lucky survivor: a large proportion of disused girder bridges have been removed for scrap

piers and trap hundreds of tiny fish between tides. Fishermen are also a common sight on the mud flats here: they come to gather cockles or to dig lugworm for bait. The whole length of the walk to Wadebridge is a haven for birdlife and a veritable treat for ornithologists. Apart from the predictable gulls, ducks and swans, there are divers, grebes, geese, plovers, terns and hawks, together with occasional rarities such as migrants blown off course.

The line now passes over Oldtown Cove before reaching the long-abandoned Penquean slate quarries (grid reference 953739). This area was a hive of activity in the seventeenth and eighteenth centuries and huge piles of slate still line the sides of the old trackbed. It is incredible to think that, in 1682/3, this derelict and desolate place supported a business which exported a million slates.

The next feature is Tregunna Bridge (grid reference 966739), which is unusual in being the only overbridge on this section. Huge pools of water used to line the trackbed here and, in May, they positively teemed with tadpoles. Unfortunately, the council has recently raised the level with rubble and, while this eliminates the wetness, it has also eliminated the tadpoles. About a mile after Tregunna, the walker meets a new road built to serve the nearby sewage-works: this has been laid along the course of the old railway and leads straight into the centre of Wadebridge.

A set of traffic lights gives controlled access across the busy A39. The walker should then continue in a south-easterly direction, past a local supermarket and through a car park which leads to Southern Way and the remains of Wadebridge railway station. After years of neglect, the main station building is now being restored as the John Betjeman Centre. This commemorates Betjeman's deep love of the Cornish countryside and a memorable passage in his autobiographical poem *Summoned by Bells*, which evokes the memory of a train journey from Waterloo to Wadebridge via Egloskerry and Tresmeer on the North Cornwall line. When complete, the restored and extended building will combine a day centre for the elderly with a social and cultural centre for the retired. The former ticket office will accommodate the John Betjeman library and memorabilia collection.

In the mid-1970s, James Winstanley was a student at Exeter. The line to Padstow had closed but freight services still ran to Wadebridge and Wenfordbridge. He has vivid recollections of travelling on these by special arrangement with British Rail's area office at Bristol:

In those days, you could pay BR a generous fee to attach one or two extra brake vans to the freight trains which ran to Wadebridge or Wenford. The Wadebridge train left Bodmin Road at five in the morning while the Wenford service left at nine minutes past nine, an altogether more civilised time which did at least offer enthusiasts from Exeter a sporting chance of getting there. I finally made it to Wadebridge on the last day of service. The weather was dreadful: cold, grey, windy and wet. A three coach diesel train growled up the branch and back: it was absolutely packed and the windows covered in condensation so that you could hardly see out – a poor substitute for the luxury of a brake van trip.

A ride in a brake van was out of this world. The train crews treated you like royalty. I remember stopping at Boscarne on one occasion and wondering what the hold up was about when the guard came round and recited the menu from the local pub. He had apparently spoken to the landlord on the phone and wanted to take orders so that our food could be ready when the train pulled up at the bottom of the hill. They used to stop at the local farms and collect produce for their wives. There were free cab rides too. The management would have gone mad about all this but some of the staff, like the Bodmin shunter, can't have seen a passenger for months. They just wanted some company, someone to talk to.

Nowadays, the empty trackbed can be picked up again at the end of Southern Way. The line from here to Wadebridge Junction (grid reference 001714) appeared to be double track but, in reality, was two parallel single lines: the northern line led to Launceston via the North Cornwall line, while the southern line led to Boscarne and the three Bodmin stations.

Polbrock Bridge from the trackbed. Given the early date of this line, it is not surprising that some of its structures have a vernacular look which is reminiscent of the canals

Shortly after Pendavey bridge (grid reference 004710), the Bodmin and Wadebridge line enters the upper reaches of the intimate, steeply-wooded Camel Valley. This is an area much loved by local fishermen, whose rods and umbrellas can sometimes be glimpsed through the trees. The age of the line is clearly revealed at Polbrock, where the vernacular architecture of an attractive overbridge owes more to the age of canals than of railways. Just west of Grogley Halt, the line passes through a rock cutting which was constructed in 1886 to eliminate a sharp curve. The simple platform of the halt still stands at grid reference 015685 and a rough track to the nearby lane follows the course of the early Ruthern Bridge branch. What is more remarkable is that the line eliminated by the 1886 cutting can still be traced from beginning to end over a hundred years after its closure: it enters the station site as a grassy track from the west.

The line now runs into Boscarne on a ledge cut into the southern slope of Penhaligon Downs, with beautiful views across the Camel Valley to isolated farms and cottages around Threewaters and Nanstallon. Nanstallon Halt remains at grid reference 034676, complete with mile and gradient posts, but the railway path comes to an abrupt end in front of buffer stops just west of Boscarne. It is not entirely clear what the walker is intended to do here but, if he carries on, he will find his way unobstructed to the now dismantled level crossing at grid reference 040675. Extensive sidings still remain here, but they are now partly dismantled and much overgrown. In James Winstanley's time, they accommodated rows of blue-hooded china clay wagons from Wenfordbridge.

The walker now has two options. He must make his way to Dunmere Junction at grid reference 046675 and can follow either the derelict railway (take the branch to the left) or a parallel footpath which runs along the embankment to the north. As the continuity of the Camel Trail is not clear at this point, the latter is probably the sensible course.

At Dunmere Junction, the Wenfordbridge branch curves away to the north-east through a gate now left permanently open, while the Bodmin North branch curves away to the east on an average gradient of 1 in 47. The present alignment is a considerable improvement on the original in terms of directness and incline but, even for a walker, it is still steep enough to be noticed. Little Dunmere Halt is passed at grid reference 047676 and it is then a straightforward climb to the site of Bodmin North station, which now accommodates a new Gateway supermarket. A few years ago, the discerning explorer could trace a few bits of platform and railway fencing on the site but these frail remnants are unlikely to have survived this wholesale redevelopment.

Further Explorations

The other obvious railway walk in the area is the Wenfordbridge branch. This hugs the east bank of the River Camel for six miles north of Dunmere and is highly picturesque, particularly around Hellandbridge (where it runs through the middle of a row of cottages) and in Helligan Wood. It is very much an early contour railway which utilized the river valley and, as such, there is hardly a straight length in it. The china clay works which supported the line for so long will be found at grid reference 083742 and a constant plume of steam reveals that it is still at work. Wet clay is pumped here for drying from mines on Stannon Moor, six miles away. While on the subject, Cornwall now has a china clay museum at Wheal Martyn, some two miles north of St Austell on the A391. This includes many buildings and artefacts from the industry and gives visitors an opportunity to understand it more fully.

For the less energetic enthusiast, the Bodmin and Wenford Railway is now based at Bodmin General station. Until August 1989, its scope had been limited to static exhibits and brake van rides in the station yard but the recently-granted Light Railway Order should change all that and have trains running again to Bodmin Parkway on British Rail's main line from Plymouth to Penzance. The railway's stock list includes a diminutive AC Cars four-wheeled railbus of the type used on services to Bodmin North in the 1960s; it is currently awaiting restoration and the fitting of a new engine.

Further to the east, the Launceston Steam Railway now runs towards Egloskerry on one and a half miles of the restored North Cornwall line. This uses a 2 ft gauge and a pair of antique Victorian steam locomotives. *Lilian* was the first to be acquired, a cabless locomotive which must make drivers dread bad weather. However, the most surprising railway relics from north Cornwall now reside in the National Railway Museum at York. These are two early vehicles from the Bodmin and Wadebridge line: a second class compartment carriage, which clearly reveals its stage-coach origins, and an alarming third class vehicle which is like a collection of church pews mounted in a coal truck. The nineteenth-century man-in-the-street could not have enjoyed much comfort in the likes of this but how wonderful that the little Bodmin and Wadebridge should be so commemorated in the nation's premier railway collection.

Transport and Facilities

Map: Ordnance Survey: Landranger Series Sheet 200 (recommended)

Buses: Western National Ltd
21a Pydar Street, Truro, Cornwall
Telephone: Truro (0872) 40404

Trains: British Rail Telephone Enquiry Bureaux
Telephone: Plymouth (0752) 221300
            or: St Austell (0726) 75671
            or: Truro (0872) 76244

The most useful bus for railway ramblers is undoubtedly Western National's service 55, which connects with British Rail trains at Bodmin Parkway. There are some nine departures a day for Bodmin, with six continuing to Wadebridge and Padstow. Following deregulation of the buses, a late service was introduced which departed from Padstow at 8.40 p.m. but it remains to be seen if this attracts enough custom to ensure its long-term survival.

As might be expected, Cornwall is not exactly overrun with buses and some of the most useful services, at least from a railway rambler's point of view, are the most difficult to track down. In 1985, I led a walk along the Wenfordbridge branch and was astonished to meet a bus in the vicinity of its northern terminus. This was probably a local service from Bodmin to St Breward and, as such, would be invaluable for anyone who wanted to walk this idyllic branch. Enquiries should be directed to the bus enquiry office listed in Appendix C or the Tourist Information Office at Shire House, Mount Folly Square, Bodmin, Cornwall, PL31 2DQ.

The county is, of course, well equipped for the tourist trade with plenty of pubs, cafés and restaurants. However, from the point of view of this walk, the only viable refreshment stops are at Padstow, Wadebridge, Dunmere and Bodmin. The Borough Arms at Dunmere is particularly convenient, being located immediately above Dunmere station at grid reference 048676. The local brewers are Devenish and St Austell; like the majority of such companies, they are the visitor's best bet for value.

The total mileage of railway paths in this area is now extensive so it may be useful to hire a bicycle. The local hire shops are Glyn Davies Bike Hire, South Quay, Padstow, telephone: Padstow (0841) 532594, and Bridge Bike Hire, Eddystone Road, Wadebridge, telephone: Wadebridge (020 881) 3050.

7
THE NEW FOREST
Cater's Cottage (Brockenhurst) to Burbush Hill (Burley)

Introduction

One of the most scenic railway routes in Hampshire runs through the New Forest from the village of Sway to what is quaintly called 'Lyndhurst Road'; the railway always resorted to this style of naming when a station was nowhere near the village whose name it bore. The fact that the railway managed to cross the New Forest at all is no small achievement on the part of its promoters and, to this day, the Forest boundary writhes around the station at Lyndhurst Road as though recoiling from contact with distant Waterloo.

Nowadays, of course, this is part of the Bournemouth main line. Even on a slow train, the ten-mile journey across the New Forest takes a mere fourteen minutes so the traveller must be very sharp-eyed to notice any evidence that, until Brockenhurst, he is travelling on a route which is a substitute for the original. But one and a half miles north-east of Sway, the evidence is there – the white spot of a crossing keeper's cottage just below the northern skyline and a long embankment, now cloaked in trees, which leads to the site of Lymington Junction. Here lines once fanned out in three directions. While those to Bournemouth and Lymington survive, the former main line to Dorchester via Ringwood and Wimborne was a victim of the Beeching axe, its last passenger train running on 4 May 1964.

History

The London and Southampton Railway reached Southampton on 11 May 1840 and its arrival triggered considerable development and expansion in the town. This railway-induced prosperity became the subject of some envy in west

Hampshire and Dorset, where landowners and other influential men began to appreciate the disadvantages of remaining off the railway map. The most significant protagonist of the railway cause turned out to be Charles Castleman, a solicitor with offices in Wimborne and Ringwood, and it was largely as a result of his energy and commitment that a line from Southampton to Dorchester was built. It opened for traffic on 1 June 1847.

It is, of course, possible to claim some self-interest in Castleman's enthusiasm, for his route appears almost to be custom-designed. The inclusion of Wimborne and Ringwood certainly made it very sinuous and this earnt it the nickname 'Castleman's Corkscrew'. Even allowing for the fact that, in the early 1840s, Bournemouth was still in its infancy, a greater population would have been served had the line been built along the present route, serving places such as Christchurch and Poole. But this is being wise after the event. The engineer, Capt. Moorsom, claimed considerable difficulties in the course of the direct line and, while this may have suited Castleman, he deserves credit for ensuring that the Dorchester scheme was soundly based. After all, these were the 'boom and bust' days of railway mania.

Notwithstanding this, the 'Corkscrew' failed to serve Christchurch, which in the 1840s was one of the major towns in the area, while the growth of Bournemouth continued to gather pace. Christchurch, being the older and more established town, was first to join the railway network, and this was achieved by means of a branch line from Ringwood which followed the course of the Avon Valley. An extension to Bournemouth was envisaged from the outset but this was deferred in 1858, perhaps because of difficulties in raising the capital. Thus, when the branch opened on 13 November 1862, passengers for Bournemouth had to travel on from Christchurch by connecting omnibus. A separate fare of 1s. 6d. was charged for this and passengers were required to add a bonus for the driver. This arrangement meant that the journey from Waterloo to Bournemouth took a typical five hours.

After a period of financial difficulty, the Christchurch line was extended to Bournemouth and opened for through traffic on 14 March 1870. Bournemouth was now a thriving town of some 5,000 souls and this extension finally secured the profits for which the railway promoters had long hoped. There were initially five return workings to Ringwood per day, but these were soon increased to six. Here Bournemouth passengers could change for east- or west-bound services on the 'Corkscrew'.

Like Jack's beanstalk, Bournemouth simply grew and grew. It is amazing, therefore, that a tenuous single-track branch line through the Avon Valley remained its main route to London for nearly twenty years. Ultimately, the little line could scarcely cope with the volume of Bournemouth traffic and connectional delays of up to forty-five minutes at Ringwood made it very unpopular. Under these circumstances, the entire Bournemouth route developed a reputation as one of the worst backwaters on the London and South Western Railway.

The important market town of Ringwood has been devoid of its railway for over a quarter of a century and no longer is it possible to board a train bound for Wimborne or Brockenhurst. Earlier still, the station had been the junction for a line through Hurn to Christchurch and Bournemouth on which services started from the bay platform just visible on the extreme left
Lens of Sutton

Unfortunately for travellers, the company was not unduly bothered as it exercised a monopoly, a situation only threatened in 1882 by a proposal from the Didcot, Newbury and Southampton Railway to construct a direct line of its own to the town. The subsequent history of the Didcot company proves this to have been a most extravagant gesture, but the directors of the LSWR could not have known this and fear of competition remained a factor behind the building of their direct line via Sway. This opened on 5 March 1888 and reduced the Waterloo to Bournemouth journey time to something under three hours. At the same time, a link was also provided across Bournemouth to Poole.

The fate of the line from Ringwood to Christchurch had been sealed. It soon assumed the mantle of a rustic branch line and puffed out of existence on 30 September 1935. 'Castleman's Corkscrew' was also diminished by the diversion of the lucrative Bournemouth traffic but a worse blow was dealt in 1893 when a short line known as the Holes Bay curve was built. This finally crossed the northern waters of Poole Harbour and provided a direct route through Bournemouth to Poole and the Dorchester line beyond. This cut-off formed the shortest route to Dorchester and made Castleman's original line via Wimborne and Ringwood a lengthy and time-consuming detour. It was thereafter a duplicate and secondary route. Forced to rely on purely local traffic, a gradual decline set in which culminated in the line's closure in 1964.

Once part of the original railway from Southampton to Dorchester, Holmsley suffered a slow decline culminating in closure in 1964. Viewed from the same vantage point today, a road passes along the trackbed while the station buildings have become a tea room. The original station at Dorchester was built facing Exeter, destination of a proposed extension

Lens of Sutton

The Line Today

The route of the 'Corkscrew' today is unusual in that a large proportion of it remains in public ownership, but no conscious effort has yet been made to convert it into a continuous railway path. From east to west, the main landowners are the Crown, Hampshire County Council, British Rail, Dorset County Council, the Ministry of Defence and Poole Borough Council. The Forestry Commission acts as agent for the Crown and manages the whole of the New Forest, including the railway walk described in this chapter. Hampshire County Council owns a portion of the trackbed from the Forest boundary to Ringwood but is reported to have sold off a few sections in recent years; a pity, as this breaks the continuity of the route. Poor old British Rail is believed still to own a succession of bridges in Ringwood which cross the River Avon; presumably no one is willing to purchase them as a going concern. Of the other landowners, Dorset County and Poole Borough councils have created a number of local cycleways along the old trackbed and these are described below.

Returning to the eastern part of the route, the Forestry Commission feels that the ability of the New Forest to accommodate ever more tourists is nearly exhausted and is concerned at soil erosion by pedestrians on many of its paths. Surely an ideal solution would be to channel some of these visitors on to the old railway? After all, it was designed to carry the impact of express passenger trains and the pounding of walkers' boots must be a small thing in comparison. The public has a general right of access in the Forest and the old railway is already used informally and extensively as a walk. With official encouragement and a few local improvements, it could become an attractive feature that takes pressure off some of the more vulnerable localities.

The Walk (7 miles)

The walker must begin by making his way to the southern extremity of Brockenhurst on the B3055. The trackbed can be gained at Cater's Cottage, which is just over a mile south-west of the village at grid reference 286994; the location is marked by the first of many former crossing keepers' cottages. The line strikes off west in a cutting through Blackhamsley Hill; this is often very wet but conditions soon improve. Once beyond the cutting, the line continues on an embankment across Hincheslea Bog. This offers extensive views of the surrounding countryside and was quite clearly the start of a most attractive railway journey. The broad sweep of the old trackbed leads invitingly into the distance.

Much of the Forest has never been cultivated and therefore never properly drained; bogs abound and walkers stray from recognized paths at the peril of waterlogged boots. During the war, the land to the south of this embankment was drained and the old irrigation channels can still be seen as grassy hollows.

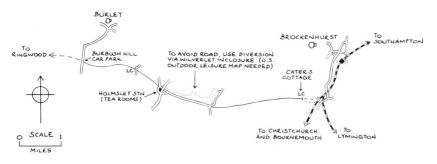

The New Forest

An attempt was made to grow cereals here but the poor quality of the soil defeated it and the land was later used for pasture. Nowadays it is fallow again but the Forest livestock keep the grass neatly cropped.

Two underbridges have been removed on this section. By carefully studying the abutments of the second, the walker can see where it was widened in 1863 to take double rather than single track. Just over a hundred years later, British Rail was unable to give the Forestry Commission any guarantees as to the bridges' long-term safety so the Commission, regrettably, allowed the railway to demolish them. As a result, walkers have to climb down and up the embankments on either side. This has had the unfortunate effect of gouging out several deep ruts, which in turn add fuel to the Commission's complaints about soil erosion. The obvious answer would be to install new lightweight pedestrian bridges; perhaps the Territorial Army could be persuaded to undertake this as a training exercise and engineering project? There is a precedent in the Peak National Park, where TA Royal Engineers constructed a new bridge over the fast flowing River Derwent at Water-cum-Jolly.

A quarter of a mile later, the line passes under an attractive triple span brick bridge which carries a minor road from Sway to Wilverley. Another smaller bridge soon follows, beyond which the walker enters Setthorns Camping Site. This is part of the Forestry Commission's provision for tourism and is considered by some to be the most attractive of all such sites in the Forest; it is certainly the perfect spot for the back-packing or caravanning railway rambler. The occasional deer has also been spotted here. Tents and caravans will normally be found on the trackbed only at the busiest times, such as the August bank holiday.

Leaving Setthorns, an attractive overbridge is crossed as the line begins a long sweeping curve to Wilverley, where an underbridge has been filled in and the old line converted into a road. This leads to Holmsley station but is best avoided as it is very straight. To put it mildly, straightness is not a characteristic of other Forest roads and motorists tend to 'open up' when they reach it. The walker is best advised to turn north for Wilverley Inclosure, which offers a pleasant detour to Holmsley by way of various woodland paths. A good map and some experience at map-reading are necessary for this, but the effort is rewarded in terms of peace and quiet, not to mention safety. The most practicable guide is the Ordnance Survey's Outdoor Leisure Map 22. Public conveniences can be found just inside the inclosure at grid reference 253007.

Holmsley station was opened as part of the main 'Corkscrew' in 1847, when it bore the name Christchurch Road. Eight wearying miles of Christchurch road then lay between station and town, but a regular omnibus service ran to Christchurch and Bournemouth's Bath Hotel for those who could afford it. Today the station has been converted into a tea room and it offers a very welcome facility. The owners are very mindful of the building's history and a selection of old railway photographs and tickets are displayed within.

Bridge west of Setthorns. As many animals as humans use the tracks which pass below. Special crossings for animals remain a feature of railways and roads in the New Forest to this day, although careless motorists inflict a terrible toll on the Forest livestock every year

Mrs Joyce Dickers is now a greengrocer at Southbourne, a coastal town just west of Christchurch, but during the war was billeted in Holmsley station. Her room was at the west end of the building and overlooked the now-demolished signal-box. As a member of the Timber Corps of the Women's Land Army, she worked at a sawmill just outside the station and was responsible for invoicing truckloads of timber. Most of this went out as pit props for the South Wales coalfield around Pontypridd or sleepers for the railway works at nearby Redbridge. These were busy days for the railway, for petrol rationing ensured a brisk passenger trade and, apart from the timber, ammunition and ambulance trains passed through from time to time. Ammunition trains to Southampton reached a peak in the build-up to D-Day in June 1944, often travelling unmarked and at night. The only evidence might be a train-load of wagons stored temporarily in a siding sheltered by trees, where the deadly cargo could not be seen from the air. The ambulance trains conveyed Allied casualties to hospitals in Ringwood and Wimborne; they would pass through with blinds drawn to prevent any demoralization at the sight of the human cost of war. In June 1944, the D-Day invasion brought this traffic to a peak and, in that month alone, the Southern Railway ran 104 ambulance trains, each of which could hold 300 men.

The Old Station Tea Rooms, formerly Holmsley and initially Christchurch Road. Modern patrons outnumber past railway passengers to such an extent that the building has twice had to be extended. The extensions (one is visible on the left of the photograph) are most sympathetically done

But ordinary life continued as well, including Mrs Dickers' courtship by her now husband, John. Somewhere in the woods around Holmsley lies the skeleton of his first motorcycle, which blew up one night rather than carry him home.

The enduring image of people who recall the railway at this time is of little engines hauling three or four coaches. Mrs Straw of West Moors recalls them at the Wimborne end of the line, where they could be seen above her garden on an embankment. They were not particularly clean; labour shortages saw to that. The compartments had string luggage racks and, if you were lucky, a door to one of the two toilets per coach. The grubby windows could be lowered by a leather strap. The few vehicles of this vintage which survive on private railways are now beautifully restored and do not convey an accurate impression of what 'the Southern' was like in those days of austerity and shortage. But the regular coming and going of the local train continued, war or not, and the Forest setting provided a beautiful background against which this withering main line could work out its time.

At modern-day Holmsley, roads around the station have been realigned and, unfortunately, one severs the former Ringwood platform. The rambler must cross this road and pass through an apparently solid hedge to regain the trackbed. However, the hedge conceals a path and stile which lead to the remains of the platform, fascinating for the industrial archaeologist.

The most obvious feature is the platform itself, a long and sturdy brick structure. At its west end, a pair of bridges cross a little stream: the larger carried the main double track and the smaller a siding. At the very end of the platform, look for a metal post in the ground perforated at regular intervals with holes. This was the mounting for a number of pulley wheels which guided various signal wires. These were led under the track just outside the station and continued for three quarters of a mile on the opposite side. The concrete posts which carried them away can still be seen, their purpose again revealed by tell-tale holes. The course of these wires can be traced to the stumps of three LSWR lattice-style signals: the starter for Ringwood, the signal for Holmsley yard and the distant for Holmsley station. Be prepared for a long walk to the last one!

Beyond the end of the platform and just over the stream, two larger metal posts still stand in the ground. The first carried a large plate bearing the bridge's number; all bridges were numbered sequentially from the start of the line. The second was a gradient post and the stumps of its two shorn limbs are still evident – level into the station and a rising gradient towards Ringwood. This discovery confirmed Mrs Dickers' recollection that a four-coach train had quite a struggle on the way to Burley, the next village near the line. On the other side of the trackbed, a large metal plate can be found just above ground level and this would have formed a pivot for some of the point rodding outside the station.

Continuing towards Ringwood, the line enters a delightful avenue of trees on a shallow embankment. A number of discarded telegraph poles can be found on the north side here; these were a product of the railway's Ashford Concrete Works and, needless to say, have not rotted, although some are now half-submerged in the marshy ground hereabouts. The line then enters open country, again with fine extensive views, and takes a broad sweep to the left before reaching gatehouse 11. This former crossing keeper's hut survives intact and once guarded the very minor lane from Burley to Holmsley Inclosure. The site is notable in that a full set of rails remains in the tarmac.

The next feature of interest is Greenberry Bridge, which conveys a minor path across the line. On hot summer days, ponies shelter here from the glare of the afternoon sun. The bridge straddles a cutting which is a favoured haunt of rabbits, as the many holes of a large warren reveal. Gorse and broom now adorn the line as it enters a particularly wild and open stretch. It is surprising, therefore, to discover the remains of gatehouses 12 and 13 within the next half mile. They are most easily spotted by their gate posts; both retain a complete set of four and one is adorned in spring with a blaze of rhododendron flowers. The real mystery is why crossings were ever constructed in these remote spots. There are certainly no modern footpaths here. The nineteenth-century Woods and Forests' Commissioners were not easy men to appease in the matter of the line's construction, so perhaps these crossings were built at their stipulation?

The end of the walk is now in view as the line enters a cutting which skirts the southern flank of Burbush Hill. A modern concrete bridge soon appears in the distance but the walker should climb the embankment to his right before reaching it. This avoids a section which is usually waterlogged. The top of the embankment can be followed with ease and a number of paths to Burbush Hill car park (grid reference 203018) soon lead off to the right. Burley village lies a mile to the north-east by way of a minor road; its facilities include public conveniences, tea rooms and gift shops, plus a limited bus service to Ringwood and Southampton.

Further Explorations

The walker should not attempt to continue from Burbush Hill to Ringwood unless he is prepared to track down the relevant landowners and obtain their permission to do so. If this section is followed, it is essential to wear wellington boots through the cutting immediately west of Burbush Hill, where the rambler will witness the unusual spectacle of water gurgling out of, rather than into, the drainage ducts. This is a very boggy area and, when dry, the soil is very light and friable; this explains the extent to which it has blocked and deranged the railway drainage.

Crossing keepers' cottages remain at Crow, Hightown and Moortown, but of Ringwood station there is no longer any trace; the whole area has recently been cleared for redevelopment, although it is not known yet what form this will take. Things improve west of Christchurch Road (grid reference 151048). The old line can be followed with ease across the Avon Valley, where there are five bridges of varying sizes, plus the remains of sundry telegraph poles and pulley posts. The A31 will be met at the end of this section, but the walker may continue by a minor road which passes safely under it. Shortly after this at grid reference 138050, the start of Dorset County Council's 'Ashley Trailway' will be found. This follows the 'Corkscrew' as far as West Moors and passes Ashley Heath station (complete with concrete sign board) *en route*.

At West Moors, the trackbed is occupied by an army depot and, obviously, access here is quite impossible. On the other side of the village, it is used as an unmade access road which serves the northern side of Ferndown Industrial Estate but, again, permission should be obtained from the relevant landowners. Anyone who does obtain permission will certainly have to stop at Canford Bottom, where a new dwelling blocks the route.

From here to Oakley (which is south of Wimborne and the site of a former level crossing), the continuity of the route has been destroyed. Wimborne station now accommodates new housing, while the girder bridge which once crossed the River Stour to its south has long been demolished. At Oakley, however, there is a dramatic improvement for the line is now used as a cycle path to Broadstone and Upton. A short tunnel is passed at Merley, where restored railway drainage still has its work cut out, but there is no trace of Broadstone station which has been replaced by a large sports centre. Just south of this spot, the former main line to Poole and Bournemouth West has been converted into a new road, but the 'Corkscrew' miraculously survives; it follows the new road south for a mile but then turns west across Upton Heath.

Dorset County Council has expressed an interest in creating a continuous path along the 'Corkscrew', including a pleasant diversion around Wimborne on the banks of the River Stour. No doubt it is too much to hope that Hampshire County Council and the Forestry Commission would join it in such a venture. But while the prospect of a 'Corkscrew Cycleway' remains a remote one, plenty of this fascinating line is still open to the public. It would take a weekend to cover its entire length but the various sections which are rights of way make very agreeable shorter rambles.

The little line from Ringwood to Christchurch has not been so lucky. Part of the trackbed has been incorporated in the new A338 Ringwood to Bournemouth trunk road, but a tiny fragment survives at Matchams View in the Avon Forest Park (grid reference 134022) and, south of Hurn station, two miles remain in use as a forest track although there is no official public access to the author's knowledge. Hurn station has been extended somewhat and now trades as the Avon Causeway Hotel (grid reference 137977). For many years, it was crammed with railway paraphernalia including posters, timetables and a liberal helping of first class compartments rescued from Mk 1 rolling stock. These actually formed part of the seating accommodation and it was rather novel that whole compartments were used, including the sliding doors. A recent refurbishment has made the establishment much more up-market but swept away all of these eccentric curiosities, except the railway carriage which still waits at the trackless platform. Considering that the line closed in 1935, it is hardly surprising that the years have so eroded it. The Avon Causeway Hotel no longer resembles a former station but, while the new owners can find a use for it, their marooned railway vehicle gives the site a slightly surrealistic atmosphere. Like so much on these abandoned lines, it only makes sense if you understand the past.

Transport and Facilities

Maps: Ordnance Survey: Tourist Map 6
Ordnance Survey: Landranger Series Sheet 195
Ordnance Survey: Outdoor Leisure Map 22 (recommended)

Buses: Wilts and Dorset Bus Company Ltd
Bus Station, Dolphin Centre, Poole, Dorset, BH15 1SN
Telephone: Poole (0202) 673555

Solent Blue Line
Hampshire House, 169/170 High Street, Southampton, SO1 0BY
Telephone: Southampton (0703) 226235

Trains: British Rail Telephone Enquiry Bureaux
Telephone: Southampton (0703) 229393
or: Bournemouth (0202) 292474

Modern bus services along the 'Corkscrew' are rather thin, which is hardly surprising in view of the remote terrain the line crossed. Even now, a winter journey along some of the Forest roads imparts a strong sense of isolation, for hardly a light can be seen. The best bet is to undertake this walk with two walkers and two cars, in which case a vehicle can be left at each end.

For anyone who cannot cajole a companion into helping, public transport can be used but it requires careful planning. Both of the above bus operators run a service X1 from Southampton to Bournemouth via Lyndhurst Road station (still rail-served), Holmsley tea rooms and the Queen's Head, Burley. Wilts and Dorset run approximately six journeys per day (Monday to Saturday) on a two-hourly frequency, while Solent Blue Line run a few competing journeys at the busier times of day. This permits walkers to travel by train to Brockenhurst, walk the old trackbed to Burley, return by bus to Lyndhurst Road and there catch a train for home. On the bus part of the journey, remember to ask for Ashurst, which is the village in which Lyndhurst Road station will be found. As can be seen, local railway names are a real trap for the unwary: Lymington Junction is in Brockenhurst, Lyndhurst Road is in Ashurst and Beaulieu Road is in the middle of nowhere!

As for refreshments, the New Forest is a popular holiday area and there is no shortage of pubs, cafés and restaurants. There is plenty to choose from in both Brockenhurst and Burley but the only intermediate facilities are at the former Holmsley station, which is now a splendid and justifiably popular tea room.

8
THE ISLE OF WIGHT
A Network in Miniature

Introduction

Anyone wishing to see a railway on the Isle of Wight today must travel from Portsmouth Harbour to Ryde Pier Head, where the comfort of a modern catamaran can be exchanged for a ride on an ancient underground train. Until 1990, the vehicles used were ex-London Transport units constructed between 1923 and 1934 but in that year, they were due to be replaced by 'modern' underground trains dating from 1938. This may not sound much of an improvement, but British Rail made such a good job of upgrading them that their antiquity is not immediately apparent. The original electric trains, to be honest, were rather grotesque when compared with the delightful antiques they replaced and there are many on the island who rue the fact that its railway has been reduced from a proper network to a solitary electrified branch 8½ miles long. However, Dr Beeching had planned to banish railways from the island completely so this survival, however diminished, is at least something to be thankful for.

The rail journey from Ryde to Shanklin passes many lost travel opportunities. At Smallbrook Junction, the line for Newport and Cowes once diverged to the west; at Brading, a cross-platform connection could be made onto the Bembridge train; at Sandown, passengers could take an alternative route to Newport via Newchurch and Merstone; while, at Shanklin, they only had to stay in their seats to continue on to Ventnor via the island's longest tunnel.

But, despite these obvious depredations, a considerable amount of the island's lost railway network survives in one form or another. An unusually high proportion of abandoned railway mileage has been incorporated into the island's network of footpaths and bridleways while, for the less energetic enthusiast, the Isle of Wight Steam Railway now flourishes at Havenstreet and has ambitious plans to relay the rails to Smallbrook. British Rail has already donated sufficient

Wroxall station on the Ryde to Ventnor line, looking south towards Ventnor. Increased traffic led the Southern Railway to provide a passing loop and down platform here in 1925. It was to survive for forty years, being closed by BR along with the section of the line from Shanklin to Ventnor in 1966

Lens of Sutton

track to complete half of this extension and, given BR's enthusiastic support, the steam railway expects to be operating from an new interchange station at Smallbrook by May 1991.

History

The Isle of Wight was rather slow to embrace the railway revolution but, after a late start, soon made up for lost ground. The first line was that from Cowes to Newport, authorized in 1859 and opened for traffic on 16 June 1862. This was followed by the present day line from Ryde (St John's Road) to Shanklin, which opened on 23 August 1864 and was extended to Ventnor on 15 September 1866. These two lines remained isolated from each other until 20 December 1875, when they were united by a new line from Smallbrook Junction to Newport. A separate branch from Sandown had opened earlier that year, but its promoters had overreached themselves and ran into financial difficulties at Pan Lane on the

Passenger facilities on the southbound platform at Baynards

The beautifully preserved Hellingly station, once the junction for a unique electric overhead railway to Hellingly Hospital

outskirts of Newport, where a viaduct was required to reach the town's station. There were considerable difficulties in raising the necessary finance and, although the viaduct was built and opened for service on 1 June 1879, it was at the expense of bankrupting the company. Passengers were not inconvenienced by this unfortunate collapse as the official receiver permitted other operators to run the Sandown to Newport services, but it is interesting to note that the troublesome viaduct had to be rebuilt in 1920.

The next major piece of railway development occurred in 1880, when the line from Ryde St John's Road was extended first to Ryde Esplanade and then to Ryde Pier Head. This was very much the result of joint efforts by the London, Brighton and South Coast Railway and the London and South Western Railway, which jointly operated services into Portsmouth and regarded the situation at Ryde as a major obstacle to developing traffic to the island. Even after a century or more of development, Ryde St John's Road is still well to the south of the town and, before the extension, visitors had to disembark on the pier and travel to the railway terminus by horse-drawn tram.

These improvements meant that they had only to embark at Portsmouth and disembark at Ryde, with barely yards to walk from train to ship and ship to train. In 1880, these arrangements must have seemed the peak of modern travelling convenience; small consolation to the thousands who would queue at Ryde years later at the start or end of their summer holidays.

A branch was opened next from Brading to Bembridge with an intermediate station at St Helens; the first trains ran on 27 May 1882. In the worst tradition of railways, all three stations were on the very edge of the communities they were intended to serve.

The West Wight line followed on 10 September 1888. This was built inexpensively and very much followed the lie of the land as costly engineering works were beyond the pocket of its proprietors, the Freshwater, Yarmouth and Newport Railway.

The Isle of Wight Central Railway actually operated the line but relations between the two companies were not good and came to a head in 1913, when Freshwater trains were barred from using the main Newport station. As a result, the Freshwater company hastily acquired second-hand locomotives and rolling stock and erected its own tin shed of a station in the town, with obvious inconvenience for passengers. This dispute was resolved the following year but the 'other' Newport station was called into service again ten years later, when the Freshwater company fell out with the newly formed Southern Railway over the purchase price of its line. Needless to say, the Southern had a more modest view of the line's worth than its proprietors.

Although it was dogged by bankruptcy (hardly surprising in view of the sparse population it served), the FYNR was a pugnacious little concern and it is difficult not to admire its fighting spirit. It also had grandiose plans, as witnessed by an extraordinary map in the 1920–1 edition of Ward Lock's *Red*

Situated at a crossroads on the island's railway system, the important station at Newport once despatched trains to Ryde, Ventnor, Freshwater and Cowes. The Cowes–Ryde line was the last to close and with it went Newport. An 02 tank is seen here at the head of a motley collection of stock so typical of the steam service right up to closure

Lens of Sutton

Guide to the Isle of Wight. This shows a proposed branch line which would have given direct access from Brockenhurst on the mainland to a railway triangle midway between Freshwater and Yarmouth. This astonishing connection was to have been achieved by a tunnel two and a half miles long, bored beneath the Solent. Had this been achieved, the recent history of the Isle of Wight might well have been rewritten – and the history of the Freshwater, Yarmouth and Newport Railway along with it. For those who still cherish the island as a delightful retreat and backwater, it is probably just as well that this scheme never materialized.

The island's railway network was completed on 20 July 1897 when the line from Merstone to St Lawrence opened, an extension to Ventnor Town following on 1 June 1900. This was actually a very long way from Ventnor town, in recognition of which the Southern Railway gave it the more honest name of Ventnor West.

The line offered passengers a pleasant but unremarkable rural ride until leaving the south portal of St Lawrence Tunnel, after which it occupied a ledge on the dramatic south Wight cliffs and offered visitors the finest views from any train window on the island.

This complete network was to last a mere fifty-two years. The essential problem with island railways was their Jekyll and Hyde character: though they might prosper during the summer months, they had to do well indeed to tide themselves through the lean winter months which followed. As motorized buses and, later, private cars began to lure away ever greater numbers of passengers, the months of sunshine and profit became unable to sustain the lines' viability.

The closures began in earnest in the 1950s. Merstone to Ventnor West was the first to go, closing on 13 September 1952; television cameras recorded its demise. No such interest attended the last trains on the Bembridge and Freshwater lines when they steamed into history on 21 September the following year. By now, the islanders were beginning to protest but it was not enough to save the Newport to Sandown line, which closed on 6 February 1956.

With this, Ryde became the focus of the island's railways, its two remaining lines radiating south to Ventnor and west to Newport and Cowes. These, at least, were granted a stay of execution but their fate was sealed with the publication of the infamous Beeching Report in 1963, which envisaged an island without any trains at all.

The line to Newport and Cowes closed on 21 February 1966 with the Shanklin to Ventnor section following shortly afterwards on 18 April; it was not even allowed the dignity of a final summer season. The remaining section from Ryde Pier Head to Shanklin, always the most viable of the island's railways, survived only as a result of vigorous local protest.

The Lines Today

At its height, the island network consisted of some forty-six route miles. The Ventnor West and Bembridge branches were sold privately but all the other lines were acquired initially by the local council, as a result of which the usual waste and carnage has been greatly reduced. At the time of writing, the disposition of lines was approximately as shown in the table overleaf.

This demonstrates that a remarkable two-thirds of the island network is still in some form or other of public use and service; would that the same were true of more closed lines on the mainland. Additionally, the island's footpaths and bridleways are well signposted and well maintained, in consequence of which its railway walks are of a standard far higher than most others in southern England.

Re-use of the Island's Railways

Type of Use	Miles	Total
Roads:		
Within Newport	1.0	
St Lawrence/Ventnor area	1.0	2.0
Railways:		
British Rail	8.5	
Isle of Wight Steam Railway	1.5	
Steam railway extension	3.0	13.0
Walks/Bridleways:		
Cowes to Newport	3.0	
Newport towards Wootton (under development)	1.5	
Sandown to Horringford	3.0	
Shanklin to Wroxall	2.5	
Shide to Blackwater	1.0	
Yarmouth to Freshwater	2.5	
Other short sections	1.5	15.0
Other:		
Agricultural, residential use, etc.	16.0	16.0
Total route miles		46.0

Walk 1 – Cowes to Newport (4½ miles)

First and foremost, it is important to state that the Cowes to Newport railway ran along the west bank of the River Medina. A useful landmark is the chain ferry that plies between East and West Cowes. This berths in West Cowes at the bottom of Medina Road, from where it is a short walk to Bridge Road and then Arctic Road, which leads directly to the start of the railway path. More adventurous spirits may wish to explore the back streets of Cowes for other railway relics. The location of Cowes station is revealed by Terminus Road but no buildings remain, the site having been converted into a playing field for use by the local school. Odd stretches can be traced behind houses as far as Mill Hill Tunnel, where the local rifle club now holds its practices; in view of this new use, the southern portal has been bricked up. A detour via Gordon Road, Mill

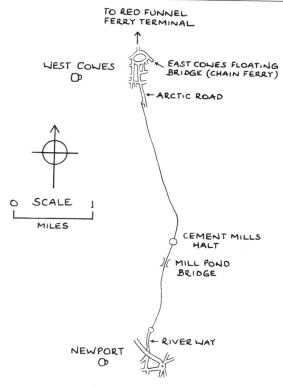

Cowes to Newport

Hill Road and Bernard Road leads to Mill Hill station, where the platform remains, though shorn of its attractive station building and flowerbeds.

Back at the end of Arctic Road, a pleasant walk awaits along the bank of the River Medina. Shortly after leaving Cowes, a track will be noticed climbing up to join the old trackbed from the left. This looks an insignificant thing now but it once gave access to Medina Wharf, the nerve centre of the island's freight traffic. This started life in 1877–8 as a timber jetty with steam cranes but was replaced in 1928 by a substantial concrete wharf on which were installed two massive transporter cranes, each with a grab capacity of one and a half tons. Nearly 150,000 tons of coal were unloaded here annually, as well as second-hand rail vehicles from the mainland which were sent across the Solent to 'modernize' the island's railway stock. Given this vast amount of traffic, Medina Wharf had extensive sidings which were often lined with ranks of wooden-sided coal wagons. Today, only a few derelict concrete lamp-posts mark the spot.

The walk could hardly be easier, as the council has laid tarmac on the old

Mill Pond Bridge between Cowes and Newport, now part of the Cowes to Newport cycleway. This is the only viaduct to survive on a closed island railway and was in a precarious state until its recent restoration

trackbed for the convenience of cyclists. This also makes it easy for the occasional tractor to rumble along on hedge-trimming duties which, ironically, are probably the first regular trackside maintenance works to be carried out since the railway closed in 1966. A number of settlement cracks appeared in the surface shortly after installation but, to its great credit, the council repaired the damage promptly. It has been rewarded with an extremely popular recreational route, as a visit on any reasonable Sunday afternoon will demonstrate.

The most notable feature visible from the line is the *Medina Queen*, an old paddle steamer moored by a marina on the opposite bank of the river where it now serves as a restaurant. It is interesting to muse that, if the line were still open, trains for Ryde would continue through Newport and pass behind the *Medina Queen* in the opposite direction – four miles by rail to travel less than one as the crow flies.

At grid reference 503917, the railway path crosses a minor concrete road. This was the site of Cement Mills Halt, a tiny platform built for the convenience of workers at the nearby West Medina Cement Works. When the works closed in 1944, the halt was retained as an unadvertised request stop and enjoyed continued use by local fishermen. In its heyday, the cement works boasted a branch from the standard gauge line and two narrow gauge tramways. One of

The Railway Medina Inn, Newport. Despite the rather contrived name, this pub is the only surviving clue as to the whereabouts of the former Newport station

these ran to the company's clay pits and passed underneath the main line just north of the halt, while the standard gauge branch diverged immediately in front of it. All this explains why the site has such an industrial appearance in the midst of an otherwise rural walk.

Mill Pond Bridge is next. This is really a low viaduct over a tributary to the River Medina and is remarkable in being the only structure of its type to survive on a closed Wight railway. As recently as 1981, it was in a rather derelict state and the railway rambler needed strong nerves to cross to the Newport side. Fortunately, the council has installed new decking and walkers may now pass in complete safety.

The last mile into Newport is uneventful. The railway path ends at grid reference 500900 where it joins a new industrial estate; the turning circle at the end of River Way marks the spot. River Way continues straight ahead and is, of course, built on the former trackbed. It makes for rather dull walking but, from a purist's point of view, is at least faithful to the old route. Orientation gets a little difficult where River Way passes under a new flyover; the only way to unravel the changes here is to make a detailed comparison of old and new maps. It is best to pass under the flyover to a point where River Way forms a T-junction with Holyrood Street. The town centre is to the right; the former railway station was immediately to the left. Little evidence remains but some of the walls hereabouts have a distinct railway look to them. The flyover follows the railway's old alignment across the River Medina, a fact probably unknown to the majority of modern car drivers.

Walk 2 – Shanklin to Wroxall (2½ miles)

Finding the start of this walk could hardly be easier – it begins immediately south of Shanklin station. Shanklin used to have a passing loop for crossing trains travelling to and from Ventnor; both tracks were electrified in 1967 but latterly the second has been removed, a victim of modern rationalization. The bridge at the south of the station suffered a similar fate. For all this, Shanklin is still an attractive town station and sympathetic redecoration by Network South East shows it off to good effect, particularly under the canopy where the finely traced initials of the Isle of Wight Railway have been highlighted in the ironwork.

The walk begins just south of the station along a new road built on the trackbed. This leads to the start of the railway path proper, from where it is a delightful walk to the centre of Wroxall.

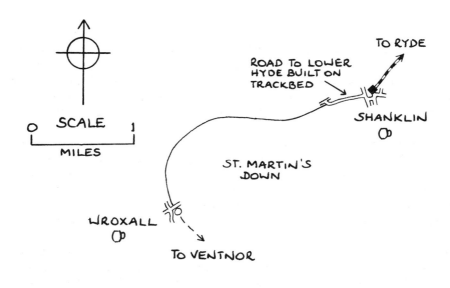

Shanklin to Wroxall

This bridge at Upper Hyde carries the A3020 over the former Shanklin–Ventnor line. This was very much the main line on the island and the depth of the cutting north of this point proves it

The first mile has a distinctly suburban feel to it as the line passes by residential roads and into a cutting which leads under an attractive bridge at grid reference 568814. After this, the line moves out into open countryside with fine views of the surrounding Downs. The excellence of the council's maintenance work is again apparent in the next cutting, where a raised causeway has been provided to remedy a waterlogged section. This looks the sort of spot where tadpoles might flourish.

The entire route is very good for wild fruit with plenty of blackberries and elderberries in evidence. Wild strawberries may also be found in the vicinity of Winstone Farm where a bridleway crosses the line at grid reference 551810. These are tiny fruits, brilliantly coloured and full-flavoured, but their diminutive size makes them an impractical proposition for any culinary use.

The line approaches Wroxall on an embankment, again with fine views of the surrounding countryside, but as the village is entered gardens have been extended across the trackbed. This usually causes a rambler's heart to sink but the excellence of the council's work is again apparent, for a wicket gate has been provided and walkers may pass on through. One of the gardens includes a small aviary inhabited by budgerigars, which add a colourful touch to the walk.

As the path nears the old station site, it leaves the trackbed and climbs the cutting bank on the west side. This leads onto an old road bridge which formerly looked down on Wroxall station. Today, no trace of the station remains. Perhaps it is time to seek consolation by heading off to The Star, Burt's fine country pub at the south end of the village.

There is no more railway path to follow, but a determined explorer may wish to walk over the Downs to Ventnor with the aid of the Ordnance Survey Outdoor Leisure Map. It is worth it for the views alone, but the north and south portals of the tunnel through St Boniface Down may still be found, together with the top of a tunnel ventilation shaft high on the hills between the two. Climbing down into Ventnor, the site of the former station (now a small industrial estate) can clearly be seen; it was built in a chalk quarry which continued in operation after the railway's opening, so the whole site was literally excavated out of the hillside.

Ventnor Tunnel opened immediately on to the station yard. When it was bored, springs were discovered which still form part of Ventnor's water supply today; the sound of gushing water can be heard clearly at the tunnel mouth. The cost of modernizing and strengthening this tunnel was one of the factors which determined the closure of this section and, besides that, a water supply and an electrified railway line are hardly comfortable bedfellows.

Walk 3 – Yarmouth to Freshwater (2½ miles)

Yarmouth is another town where the former railway station was right on the edge of development; modern visitors could be forgiven for thinking that it never had a railway in the first place. The situation was slightly better at Freshwater, but the line really needed to penetrate another mile to the west to tap the potential traffic at Totland. As it was, it ended in a no man's land which was convenient neither for Totland nor Freshwater Bay.

On arrival at Yarmouth, the walker must head for the south of the town, keeping to the east bank of the River Yar. Mill Road leads to an estuary path which gives access to the old railway, while Station Road (a turning off Mill Road) leads predictably to the old station, which is now a youth club. This may be a modest affair but it was attractively designed and its new owners keep it in good repair. The platform even boasts a modern seat, which serves as a clear reminder of the building's original purpose. The station once had a passing loop and a second platform staggered to the east, but nothing remains of them today.

On the Newport side, the railway path can be followed for just under half a mile to the site of Thorley Road bridge (grid reference 364897), but most walkers will wish to travel west to Freshwater. This is a delightful walk along

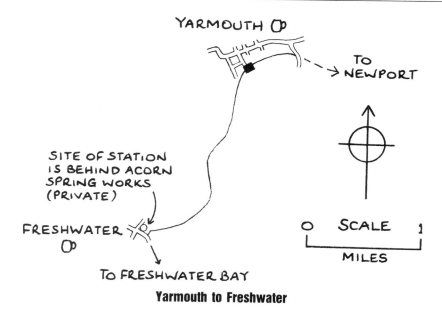

Yarmouth to Freshwater

the estuary of the River Yar, with ample opportunity for spotting a variety of waders and dippers. It is also worth looking back to Yarmouth from time to time for the view of the receding town and the broad sweep of the old trackbed.

The gradients were far gentler here than on other stretches of the Freshwater line, but some of the changes are still visible to the naked eye. It is surprising that, after so many years of closure, the line still has a railway atmosphere, with odd bits of railway fencing still visible by the trackside.

There is no particular landmark at the half-way point, but it is worth noting that this is where the Freshwater, Yarmouth and Newport Railway had intended its Solent Tunnel to join the branch, with separate junctions facing both north and south.

Just short of Freshwater station, the railway path comes to an abrupt end and swings left to join the nearby A3055. The grounds of the Afton Garden Centre now block the route but at least its proprietors have provided a convenient 'End of the Line Café' where walkers can obtain refreshments. Alternatively, the site of the old station can be reached by turning right at the main road and then right again into Hooke Hill. The Acorn Spring Works now stands on the site of the old station, which was probably the most substantial of the FYNR's buildings. A footpath runs east alongside the spring works and, from this, a length of concrete fencing can be viewed which once stood at the back of the station's platform. Even in November, this was very overgrown and it may be quite invisible during the summer months.

Further Explorations

As can be seen from the table on p. 108, there are still plenty of railway walks for the reader to explore but, if these do not appeal, it is interesting to investigate the remains of other lines from roads and footpaths – particularly the Merstone to Ventnor West branch. With the exception of Merstone, all the station buildings survive as private residences (please do not intrude on the owners' privacy) and over half the trackbed from St Lawrence to Ventnor West has been used for residential roads. This means that it is still possible to savour something of the views formerly enjoyed by rail travellers on this little-known island branch.

Really dedicated enthusiasts will find that they can locate the southern portal of St Lawrence Tunnel from a very steep footpath over the downs, but it is far too overgrown to be viewed or photographed. However, things are rather different at the northern portal, thanks to the efforts of Mr David Franks, owner of the Whitwell Mushroom Farm. Mr Franks first became interested in growing mushrooms as a commercial crop in 1951 when he was training in a nursery, but it was not until 1983 that the opportunity arose for him to start a mushroom farm of his own. St Lawrence Tunnel offered a well constructed, ready-made building which enabled him to go into production very rapidly.

All this, of course, glosses over the problem of re-establishing access to the site; anyone who has viewed the southern portal of the tunnel will appreciate this only too well. Trees some 30 ft tall were growing along the trackbed and a lot of tipping had gone on, such that the soil inside the tunnel mouth was up to 4 ft deep. It took six weeks for a digger, assisted by two tractors and trailers, to sort this lot out, after which light, heat and water supplies had to be installed. Nowadays, things are very different. The tunnel is producing one and a half tons of mushrooms per week and, while most of the crop is sold through a local wholesaler, there is a reasonable trade at the door. The farm is open five and a half days per week and will be found off the Whitwell road at grid reference 525771, the site of the only level crossing on the branch. Mr Franks' prices represent excellent value for money and a purchase offers an ideal opportunity to view the tunnel at close quarters.

Finally, mention must be made of the excellent Isle of Wight Steam Railway. Unlike many preserved railways on the mainland which, understandably, use carriages recently withdrawn by British Rail, this company's locomotives and rolling stock are all of great antiquity; but then, of course, the island's railways always were! It is invidious to single out favourites but carriage 46, the company's first class vehicle, is an historic four-wheeler constructed at Bow Works in 1864. It has been sumptuously restored and a first class supplement is keenly recommended; the interior is more reminiscent of stage-coaches than trains and a journey in it is not quickly forgotten.

All in all, the island remains a fascinating place for the railway rambler because so much of the old network remains. There is far more to relate than space permits here but, if this has whetted the appetite, readers can make a pleasant voyage of discovery for themselves.

Transport and Facilities

Maps: Ordnance Survey: Landranger Series Sheet 196
Ordnance Survey: Outdoor Leisure Map 29 (recommended)
Estate Publications: Isle of Wight Town Plans

Buses: Southern Vectis Omnibus Company Ltd
Nelson Road, Newport, Isle of Wight, PO30 1RD
Telephone: Isle of Wight (0983) 522456

Trains: British Rail Telephone Enquiry Bureau
Telephone: Portsmouth (0705) 825771

Ferries: Sealink UK Ltd
Portsmouth Harbour, Portsmouth, PO1 3EU
Telephone: Portsmouth (0705) 827744

Red Funnel Services
12 Bugle Street, Southampton, SO9 4LJ
Telephone: Southampton (0703) 226211

The island is a compact place and therefore none of these routes are of great length; this makes it quite possible to walk out and back along any of them without fear of exhaustion or wearing out one's boots. However, faint hearts will be pleased to hear that the island has an excellent bus service, even in winter, and in summer months some routes still enjoy the luxury of a conductor – a type of public servant who is almost extinct elsewhere in southern England. On the other hand, if you're not prepared to wait for the bus, the distances are all modest and this makes it quite reasonable to hire a taxi if you are walking with two or three companions.

Being a tourist island, the Isle of Wight is well endowed with pubs and eating places so few problems should arise in finding refreshments. Due to a spate of takeovers in the 1960s, most of the pubs now belong to a single brewing giant but special mention must be made of Burt and Company, a tiny family concern which still brews at Ventnor. The original brewery was hit by enemy action in

January 1943 and the damage was severe enough to deprive Wight men of its products until February 1944. A complete rebuild followed after the war with the result that a splendid agreement of 1850 still remains in force. This guarantees the owner of the Ventnor Brewery sole right to a spring supply of water for an annual rental of six old pence (2½p) – for a thousand years. Even the most avid devotee of beer must admit that water is its primary ingredient but Burts pay a lot less for it than their competitors, a benefit which they pass on to patrons of their pubs in the form of extremely reasonable prices.

9
THE DOWNS LINK
Guildford to Bramber

Introduction

Christ's Hospital station on British Rail's Mid-Sussex line enjoys a flurry of early morning and evening commuter trains but, apart from that, its rustic tranquillity is disturbed only occasionally by a stopping train from Bognor Regis to Victoria or vice versa. There is not much to the station nowadays and it offers the passenger little comfort in bad weather. A white-tiled subway links the two platforms which feature a simple brick building on the down side and an old LBSCR signal-box on the up. However, the seasoned investigator of old railways will notice a spaciousness about the site which reveals something of its past. On the west side, three platforms which once served Guildford trains now moulder away beyond the modern boundary fence while, to the east, the present-day car park used to accommodate two more platforms and the main station building. All this reveals that a very lavish structure once stood here.

In days gone by, the rail traveller could leave Christ's Hospital in no less than four separate directions and the railway authorities believed that it would develop into a major junction serving a wide range of towns and villages throughout West Sussex. The magnificent former station was constructed at the very beginning of the twentieth century in anticipation of major residential development, which never happened, and the relocation from London of Christ's Hospital School, which did. However, the school then decided to take boarders only and this further dented the railway's optimistic expectations of traffic.

The lines to Guildford and Shoreham closed on 14 June 1965 and 7 March 1966 respectively, demolition of the station following in 1972/3; the modern railway often refers euphemistically to this activity as 'rationalization'. Fortunately, West Sussex County, Surrey County and Waverley Borough councils acquired both trackbeds shortly afterwards and gradually converted them into the Downs Link, so called because it links the North Downs Way at St Martha's Hill in Surrey with the South Downs Way at Steyning in West Sussex; the

The importance of Christ's Hospital as a junction for the Guildford, Pulborough and Shoreham lines led to the development of a station somewhat out of keeping with the size of the nearby village. The main buildings were also unusual in that they mirrored the architecture of the local public school. Note the total absence of passengers in this view

Lens of Sutton

county boundary is crossed on the diversion over Baynards Tunnel. With the recent closure of the freight line from Shoreham to Beeding Cement Works, the path could be extended still further and West Sussex County Council has made the necessary approaches to British Rail which is 'reviewing' the situation. This extension is seen as a key point in increasing use of the route and it is to be hoped that British Rail's review comes to a favourable conclusion.

Unfortunately, there are a few wet and muddy stretches at the Sussex end of the walk and, although these are short, the well-prepared rambler would be wise to equip himself with a pair of wellington boots for use 'in case of need' – even in good weather. Despite this, the Downs Link has the distinction of being England's longest railway path and, in the Adur Valley, passes through some beautiful countryside.

History

A. *Christ's Hospital to Shoreham:* The earliest proposals for a railway through the Adur Valley date from 1846; various pioneers, including Robert Stephenson, saw it as a convenient corridor through which to build a line from

London to Brighton. The route offered easier construction and lesser gradients than the main line finally built through Clayton Tunnel but, despite this, it was not until 1857 that any scheme took a firm root. In that year, as if to make up for lost time, two rival schemes were presented in Parliament. A nominally independent company sought to construct a line from Dorking to Horsham and Shoreham, but made it quite clear that it hoped for the support of the London and South Western Railway. The rival London, Brighton and South Coast Railway understandably viewed this as a potential threat to its hold on the Brighton area and countered with a separate scheme for a line from Itchingfield Junction (just south of Christ's Hospital) to Shoreham via Henfield and Steyning. In the ensuing parliamentary struggle, the LBSCR emerged victorious and its bill received the Royal Assent on 12 July 1858.

The line was built very rapidly. The section from Shoreham to Partridge Green opened on 1 July 1861, that from Partridge Green to Itchingfield Junction following on 16 September of the same year. Other stations were provided at Southwater, West Grinstead, Henfield, Steyning and Bramber, a generous provision which was never altered throughout the line's history. It was originally laid as single track but was doubled between 1877 and 1879, the company perhaps hoping to develop it as an alternative route to Brighton. If so, its hopes were never realized and the line remained a typical Victorian branch throughout its existence, never attaining more than a purely local significance.

The transport historian Edwin Course believes that the line's survival ultimately depended on its being electrified as an alternative route to Brighton, but it was left out of the 1938 Mid-Sussex electrification plans and this effectively sealed its fate. Post-war plans were never implemented and the line gradually faded away; it even acquired the unsavoury nickname of the 'linger and die' line.

Given the generally unprofitable nature of the branch, it is remarkable that two wildly optimistic schemes of 1864 sought to join it at Steyning and West Grinstead, one running in from Hardham on the Mid-Sussex line, the other from Haywards Heath via Cuckfield. These schemes soon sank into oblivion and it is difficult to see how their lines could have prospered, duplicating the coastal route and having few, if any, substantial centres of population.

Steyning was always the most important centre on the line. Even in 1962, an early Brighton train started here, counterbalanced by a late northbound working the previous night. A weekly market was held just outside the goods yard and, in the early years, this was an important source of traffic. Elsewhere, however, the picture was not so good. The northern stations at Partridge Green, West Grinstead and Southwater served small communities and were all small revenue-earners, although a brickworks at Southwater brought some traffic on to the line. The only other significant industrial business came from the cement works at Beeding, which retained a rail connection until 1981.

With its rural façade belying the fact that it is a railway building, this is the approach to Slinfold station on the former LBSCR line from Christ's Hospital to Guildford

Lens of Sutton

By the 1950s, passenger traffic north of Steyning had become very light. The freight traffic must have been even worse, for all goods depots were closed in May 1962. In May 1964, modern diesel electric units replaced steam on the surviving passenger services but, seven months later, the axe fell on every signal-box bar Steyning. The last advertised service ran on 7 March 1966, followed by a recovery train which collected all re-usable station furniture. A second recovery train ran in the autumn to collect all the lineside permanent way huts and the track lifting then began in earnest. A single track was retained over the southernmost two and a half miles to serve the cement works at Beeding, but this became disused in 1981 and has since been removed. The general consensus of opinion among writers is not that the Adur Valley line should have closed but that it should have survived long enough to be closed by Dr Beeching.

B. Christ's Hospital to Guildford: The Horsham and Guildford Direct Railway was the grand name given to a company which, in the end, helped to construct another line of purely local significance. Its Parliamentary Act was passed on 6 August 1860; this authorized a line from Guildford to Stammerham (now Christ's Hospital) with a triangular junction at Stammerham which would enable the through running of trains from Guildford to either Horsham or the Sussex coast via the newly-created Adur Valley line. Unfortunately, the company's contractor experienced many problems in constructing the line and went bankrupt with losses of over £30,000. The London, Brighton and South Coast Railway took over the incomplete works in 1864, seeing a through line from Guildford to Shoreham as a potential route from the Midlands to the south coast resorts. In the event, it did not develop as such.

The LBSCR completed the line in 1865, but then the Railway Inspector refused to accept the siting of Rudgwick station on a gradient of 1 in 80. He insisted that this be reduced to 1 in 130 and, as a result, the line south of the station had to be embanked still further. The original formation included a bridge over the River Arun which now had to be raised by several feet. The solution adopted was to build a second bridge on top of the first, which created a most unusual spectacle from the level of the river. This unique double bridge survives to this day and is now used as the official emblem of the Downs Link path.

Train services commenced on 2 October 1865, but the building of Rudgwick station was not completed until two months later. The railway authorities then discovered that their expectations of traffic had been rather optimistic and fare increases followed within eighteen months. Next, perhaps inspired by the fear that the rival London and South Western Railway might obtain running powers over the line and thus gain access to the lucrative south coast resorts, the LBSCR removed the south facing spur at Stammerham on 1 August 1867. Few trains had passed over it and this forced future south-bound excursions from Guildford to travel to Horsham and reverse there.

When the line opened, Baynards was the only crossing place although two others followed, at Bramley in 1876 and Cranleigh in 1880. This reveals the fact that the northern stations on the line were always more important for traffic, although the value of Baynards was somewhat accidental. The station was originally provided to secure the support of the then owner of nearby Baynards Park but it developed a considerable goods traffic, much of it to and from a local works. Goods inward included sulphur, tin ingots and packaging materials, while goods outward ranged from bricks and fullers earth to seed dressings and polishing compounds.

In 1896 and 1898, there were plans to provide Cranleigh with a direct rail link to the north, joining the Dorking–Horsham line near Holmwood. Both failed, but such a line would have provided Cranleigh with a direct route to London. This raises all sorts of interesting speculations. Cranleigh developed as a commuter centre between the wars and, given the added stimulus of a direct route to London, might have become important enough for such a line to survive the Beeching closures. Without this, however, the history of the Horsham to Guildford branch remained one of expectations not lived up to. The railway strike of 1955 delivered a serious blow from which it never recovered. Much freight traffic deserted the line for good, as the situation at Baynards reveals all too clearly: in 1948, 802 loaded wagons were sent out but, in 1962, this figure had collapsed to one.

When the closure proposals came in 1963, they were hardly a surprise. Two years later, the only significant traffic was the eighty or so season ticket holders who travelled from Cranleigh to London but, at the TUCC inquiry held at Cranleigh Village Hall, it was apparent that many other commuters preferred to drive to Guildford rather than use the branch-line train. On top of this, the Portsmouth main line at the Guildford end was extremely busy and railway planners were probably having difficulty in finding paths for the eight or so daily Horsham trains. The die was loaded against the line's survival.

The last train left Guildford on 14 June 1965 at 6.55 p.m. and returned one hour thirty-nine minutes later. The following day, the Locomotive Club of Great Britain ran an enthusiasts' special over the line and, the day after that, the last wagons were removed from Baynards to Horsham. This was positively the last normal working over the line and, with it, yet another country railway was abandoned to the ravages of nature and time.

The Line Today

Following closure of the lines from Christ's Hospital to Guildford and Shoreham, West Sussex County Council was interested in acquiring part of the trackbed for a new Steyning/Bramber bypass but, when British Rail offered the entire route at an attractive price, conceived the idea of creating a long-distance bridleway along it. The method employed was to buy the land, dedicate a public bridleway over it and then sell it off to adjoining landowners, this arrangement being justified (in the council's view) by the route's remoteness. All things considered, the railway formation has survived this policy remarkably well, but it contains inherent dangers. These are well illustrated between Slinfold and Christ's Hospital, where landowners (as is their right) have infilled cuttings and absorbed the railway back into fields, leaving only a beaten boundary path. The walker is still allowed to pass, of course, but the resultant path is hardly distinguishable from any other. The county council's literature promotes the Downs Link as having 'industrial history interest', so it is rather worrying to think that the very features which visitors might come to enjoy could gradually disappear.

By the council's own admission, use of the Downs Link is light, yet for much of its thirty miles the sounds of civilization are never far away; it only really becomes remote in the Adur Valley. The light use may have less to do with the remoteness of the area than with the fact that the council has provided a very basic facility, a point which John Grimshaw and Associates revealed when reporting for the Department of Transport in 1982. The Sussex part of the route certainly feels as if it ought to be better used and the provision of a really good, all-weather path would go a long way towards achieving that aim. The Cranleigh and District Conservation Volunteers, who work at the Surrey end of the line, have shown what can be done. They have a regular programme of tree coppicing to improve drainage and create vistas, and they have also constructed a completely new section of path along the embankment south of Baynards Tunnel which enables walkers to avoid the muddy bridleway in the cutting. This is just the sort of community-based scheme which could help to develop and consolidate the rest of the Downs Link.

Most of the problems on the route are explained by the fact that the council's motive in purchasing the line was not primarily recreational and, naturally, any criticisms have to be viewed in the light of this historical perspective. It is highly unlikely that the same decisions would be taken now, some twenty years later. Happily, a countryside ranger has recently been appointed to manage and develop the route and, with the assistance of volunteers and other bodies, progress is being made in achieving its potential. We should all enjoy a considerably better walk in the future.

Walk 1 – Peasmarsh to Christ's Hospital (15½ miles)

The path begins at grid reference 000462, an awkward spot to the south of Shalford where the busy A281 crosses the line at the site of an infilled bridge. There is very little parking here, although a few dedicated ramblers make do along the minor lane opposite. The character of the walk is very soon established as a tree-lined path alongside a variety of waterways, natural and man-made. Fishermen can be spotted through the trees with their rods, umbrellas and green waterproofs.

Just below Chinthurst Hill, the main course of the Downs Link joins the old line at grid reference 005457; this leads south from the North Downs Way and is notable for crossing a now empty aqueduct which once formed part of the Wey and Arun Canal. More relics of the Wey and Arun are met later on and, surprisingly, a trust was set up in 1970 to promote its restoration as a navigational waterway; some small sections are reported already to have been restored. The canal is a part of London's 'lost route to the sea' and this must account for some of the enthusiasm it attracts. The trust publishes a useful guide which describes a route from Guildford to Amberley, following the old canal towpath wherever possible; copies can be obtained from the address in Appendix A.

Bramley and Wonersh station is met at grid reference 010451. A goods shed

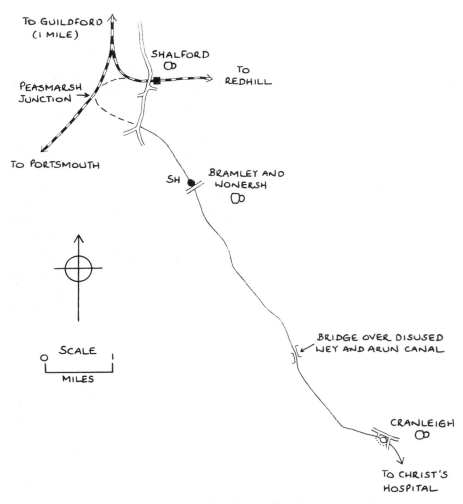

TO GUILDFORD
(1 MILE)

SHALFORD

TO
REDHILL

PEASMARSH
JUNCTION →

TO PORTSMOUTH

SH
BRAMLEY AND
WONERSH

SCALE

MILES

BRIDGE OVER DISUSED
WEY AND ARUN CANAL

CRANLEIGH

TO CHRIST'S
HOSPITAL

Peasmarsh Junction to Cranleigh

survives, now in industrial ownership, along with two platforms shaded by
many years' growth of trees. Each sports a concrete nameboard, that on the
northern platform pleasingly repainted in black and white. Opposite, a small
part of the former station building survives, albeit in rather round-shouldered
and forlorn condition.

The abandoned canal keeps the old railway company for the next few miles,
although there is usually little to see of it. However, this changes just west of
Rowly village at grid reference 035412 where the railway crosses the canal on a
very long skew bridge. The angle of the crossing is so slight that the walker

The nameboard at Bramley and Wonersh station. This could almost be a scene from an operational railway, but on turning round the walker will see nothing but deserted platforms and an empty trackbed between them

could be forgiven for thinking that the railway builders had absentmindedly constructed two entirely separate brick walls; these are the parapets. From the level of the canal, the bridge must look like a tunnel but it is impossible to confirm this suspicion as the canal bed is now strictly private. While in this area, the walker should also keep an eye out for the watercress which grows alongside the line in the old railway drainage ditches.

Just north of Cranleigh, a concrete signal post remains in place but the walker would be mistaken if this raised hopes of discovering something of Cranleigh station. The site now accommodates a rather unattractive modern shopping development, the former station yard having become the shoppers' car park. Cranleigh is one of those places whose inhabitants insist on referring to it as 'the village' despite extensive modern development – a handy conceit in view of its claim to be the largest village in England! The station was extremely well sited, with the result that the railway path still passes within a short distance of the attractive tree-lined High Street and all the usual amenities – very convenient for anyone who wants to stop here and return by bus. The path continues south past Cranleigh Recreation Centre and playing fields, after which another signal post is encountered, this time complete with a truncated signal arm, much in need of a fresh coat of paint. The Cranleigh Conservation Volunteers hope that they can

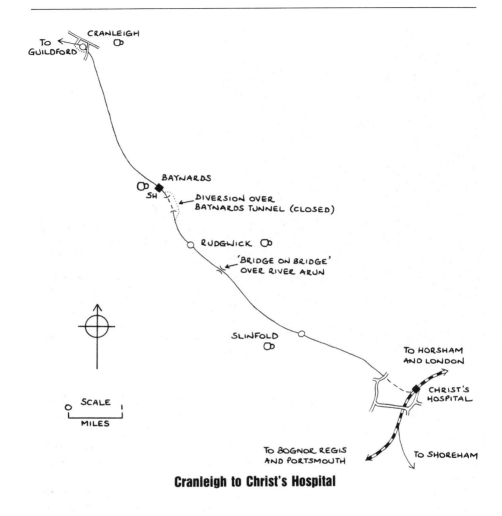

Cranleigh to Christ's Hospital

persuade a local railway modelling club to restore it to its former glory. An interesting bridge is crossed at grid reference 061379 which reveals extensive buttressing and reinforcement; once, no doubt, a railway engineer's nightmare. Local children use this section extensively, charging up and down on their bicycles.

Baynards station is the next feature of interest and is the *pièce de résistance* of the entire walk. All the other stations have been demolished and, at some, practically nothing remains. Miraculously, Baynards is entirely intact: the station building, passenger shelter, goods shed and canopies are all complete and extremely well cared for. The goods shed now accommodates a restored London Transport double-decker bus, while a vintage lorry shelters under the main canopy. The owner is reputed to be not so much a railway enthusiast as a

The remarkable 'double bridge' over the River Arun between Rudgwick and Slinfold. The nineteenth-century Railway Inspector refused to authorize the line for public use until the gradient in Rudgwick station had been eased. Unfortunately, Rudgwick station was approached by a long embankment from the south and raising it necessitated the novel provision of one bridge on top of the other

man with a love of all things old; this remarkable collection certainly underlines the point. The station has recently received an award for its contribution to local industrial archaeology but the entire site is privately owned and walkers must therefore not trespass. The nearby Thurlow Arms houses a more accessible collection of old artefacts together with a good range of ales and a very imaginative menu.

The cutting leading to Baynards Tunnel has been filled in but the site of the northern portal is marked by a concrete vent which protrudes just above the level of the ground. This was provided to ensure that the tunnel is aired and does not deteriorate unnecessarily. The present inhabitants are a small population of bats and they no doubt appreciate the thoughtful provision of extra ventilation. The diversion above the tunnel is well waymarked and rejoins the trackbed just south of the southern portal. In passing, it is worth noting that in spring the whole section from here to Slinfold is a splendour of primroses and bluebells.

The station site at Rudgwick is evident enough from a clearing but a modern health centre has replaced the old railway building. A tiny fraction of the goods platform is visible by the bridge which carries the B2128 over the trackbed but there is further evidence of the station's history a mile further on. South of

Rudgwick, the line crosses the A281 and runs along a high embankment, peppered with rabbit burrows, before reaching the remarkable double bridge (grid reference 094327) described in the history section. Slinfold Nature Reserve is arrived at next; this is a haven for all manner of wildlife including deer, woodpeckers and Purple Emperor butterflies. The station once stood at grid reference 113310 but the building has been demolished and replaced with a caravan site.

Unfortunately, the remainder of the path from Slinfold to Christ's Hospital (about two and a half miles) is something of a disappointment and most walkers could be forgiven for stopping here and transferring to the bus. On leaving the village, farmers have regraded the line and, although a path survives, it offers no clue as to its railway origin; then a cutting has been infilled and the walker must do his best on a muddy and uneven surface roughened still further by horseriders and motor-bike scramblers. The council needs to do more about this latter problem than simply declaring a prohibition: some barriers of the type used by Sustrans Ltd would be a big help. Half a mile west of Christ's Hospital, the Downs Link abandons the old trackbed altogether and takes to the nearby lanes. The route is clearly waymarked but this desertion tells its own sad tale.

Walk 2 – Christ's Hospital to Bramber (14½ miles)

The route from Guildford to Christ's Hospital was always wooded, even in the days of the railway, as many old photographs of trains on the line reveal. Given that little systematic clearing of vegetation has taken place since the last train ran in June 1965, it is hardly surprising that, for most of his journey, the walker passes through a long avenue of trees. Happily, the section from Christ's Hospital to Bramber includes some attractive downland views and offers a welcome change for anyone covering the whole of the Downs Link. The price for this, alas, is a paucity of railway relics, as demolition contractors have been busy at all of the stations.

The walk starts near the main gates of Christ's Hospital School at grid reference 146287; a fingerboard points towards the nearby Mid-Sussex line which is followed as far as Itchingfield Junction, where the old trackbed is joined. Once again, the waymarking is of a high standard and walkers will have no difficulty in keeping to the route, especially if they obtain a copy of the council's route guide.

At Southwater, two empty platforms survive at grid reference 157263 but the station buildings have been demolished; they were among the last on the line to go but the village has grown considerably since 1966 and the site is presumably

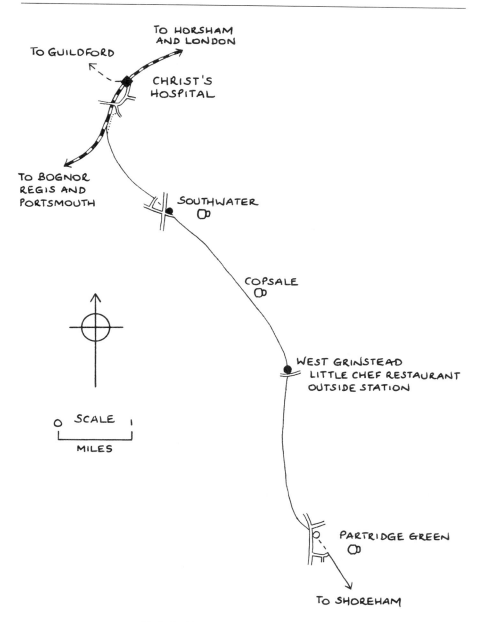

Christ's Hospital to Partridge Green

required for redevelopment. The brickworks which for many years sustained the railway here have themselves now passed into history, but their huge clay pit to the south of the line has been turned into an attractive leisure lake. This is part of Southwater Country Park, which includes refreshment facilities, public conveniences and an information centre – all very handy for passing ramblers. After the line closed, the brick company installed a network of conveyor belts in the area but these too have vanished without trace.

There is rather more at West Grinstead where the platforms are backed by high retaining walls, but the station buildings had to be sacrificed recently when the adjoining bridge on the A272 was widened; by way of compensation, the Downs Link was provided with a convenient underpass which ensures that there is no break in continuity. Two railway houses survive in the vicinity but the old station inn, deprived of its custom, has surrendered to the inevitable and been turned into a Little Chef roadside restaurant. Partridge Green station has vanished without trace, submerged beneath a new industrial estate. The approach to the village was marred by two short stretches of mud and waterlogging respectively but, hopefully, the county surveyor will attend to these when he carries out his next review of the route.

By the time Henfield is reached, the views are beginning to open out. The River Adur is crossed to the north and south of the town and the walker has good cause to be grateful for the survival of these bridges: without them, the continuity of the route would be broken and very difficult to make good. Henfield is a sizeable place to be without a railway service and its inhabitants could be forgiven for wondering at the good fortune of smaller communities on the Mid-Sussex line which still enjoy an hourly service. The station has long been demolished and replaced with a small housing estate named 'Beechings'. The name may be apt but the developers can hardly be applauded for their originality, as other roads in identical situations throughout the country reveal; Itchen Abbas in Hampshire is but one example.

South of Henfield, the rambler reaches the most attractive part of the entire walk with extensive views along the northern ridge of the South Downs. To the west, Chanctonbury Ring is clearly visible (much battered by the 1987 hurricane) while, to the east, the view extends towards Devil's Dyke. Herons may be seen here fishing in the river and irrigation ditches while, in winter, flocks of wildfowl feed and roost on the surrounding meadows. Local beef and dairy farmers sometimes leave piles of used straw bedding by the side of the line which, on cold winter afternoons, just sit there steaming – the only sign of warmth in an otherwise icy landscape. This unusual effect is explained by the fact that the used bedding is rich in FYM – farmyard manure!

The Downs Link leaves the old railway formation just over a mile north of Steyning (grid reference 195133) and gains access to Bramber via footpaths and bridleways. It is always disappointing to leave the trackbed short of one's destination, but the county council accidentally sold the intervening section to a

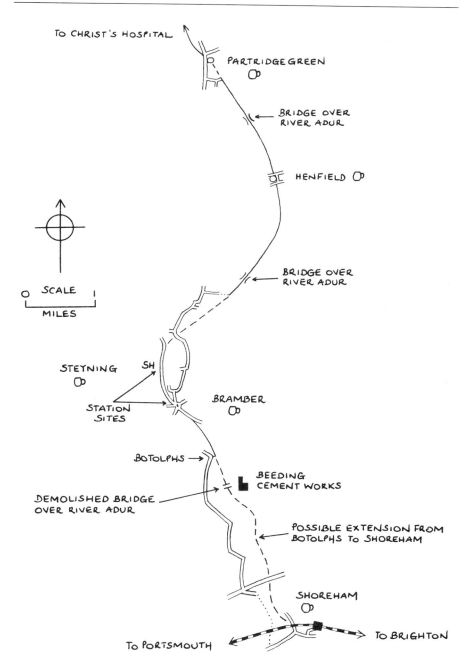

Partridge Green to Bramber

local farmer before establishing the right of way; hence the diversion. As a result, Steyning is not on the direct line of the Downs Link although it was on the original railway, a rather odd situation which causes many walkers to miss it. This is an unfortunate oversight, for it is a delightful village justly famous for the medieval timber-framed buildings in its High Street, an understandably popular subject with artists. The railway used to skirt around the east of Steyning before reaching Bramber, whose station stood in an imposing position below the remains of Bramber Castle. This stretch of the line is now busier than ever, having been turned into a bypass for the two villages. As a result, little trace remains of their respective stations, save for the goods shed at Steyning (grid reference 182113), a rare survivor considering the demolition of most other railway buildings on the line.

South of Bramber, a local farmer has kindly allowed the path to be extended along the trackbed as far as the tiny hamlet of Botolphs, where the Downs Link finally meets the South Downs Way just north of St Botolph's Church. This is the end of the official railway walk. The last few miles into Shoreham survived for many years as a long siding which served the Blue Circle cement works at Beeding, but this has recently been closed and lifted. The familiar rumours of a preserved railway circulated for a while but, in the end, came to nothing. It would be easy to extend the railway path to the coast at Shoreham were it not for the demolition at Beeding of a third bridge over the River Adur, which effectively isolates the two sections of line on opposite banks. This obstacle could prove to be insurmountable but it is appealing to muse over the possibility of a railway path connecting the coastal conurbation with the South Downs Way. Its creation depends ultimately on the outcome of negotiations between West Sussex County Council and British Rail.

Further Explorations

Anyone who has walked the entire thirty miles of this path may feel a little weary for further exploration and, in a sense, this is just as well for there are relatively few other railway- or even canal-oriented attractions in the area. The only railway walks which could be described as local are the Worth Way and Forest Way which together provide a through route from Three Bridges (one mile west of Crawley) to East Grinstead and Groombridge. Both of these, particularly the Forest Way, are attractive walks and it is a known fact that the county council owns and maintains the trackbed of the Worth Way, for it has been closed in the past to enable damage by horses to be repaired.

On the canal side, mention has already been made of the Wey and Arun Canal Trust and its guide to the old towpath from Guildford to Amberley. On a similar theme, West Sussex County Council publishes a small guide to the towpath of the Portsmouth and Arundel Canal, which can be followed from Ford to Chichester or Birdham. Chichester was served by a short branch off the main cut and this, together with the section from Hunston to Birdham, are still water-filled – albeit somewhat weed infested.

The nearest preserved railway is the famous Bluebell line which runs from Sheffield Park (five miles west of Haywards Heath) to Horsted Keynes. This is the grandfather of preserved railways and has high hopes of extending northwards to East Grinstead. Further south on the coast at Brighton, Volk's Electric Railway (now in the care of the town council) still trundles back and forth between Palace Pier and Black Rock. Back in the country, another interesting feature is the Amberley Chalk Pits Museum, located just outside Amberley railway station. This houses a growing collection of industrial artefacts from south-east England's industrial past, including a number of vintage buses and narrow gauge industrial railways. The museum also stages occasional demonstrations of boat-building, printing, smithing and other craft skills using authentic preserved equipment.

Transport and Facilities

Maps: Ordnance Survey: Landranger Series Sheets 186, 187 and 198
The Downs Link Route Guide (recommended)

The route guide is published by the local authorities listed below. When ordering, please enclose a cheque or postal order for 50p to cover the cost of the guide plus post and packing:

Surrey County Council
County Hall, Penryn Road, Kingston-upon-Thames,
Surrey, GU7 1HR
Telephone: 01–546 1050

Waverley Borough Council
The Burys, Godalming, Surrey, KT1 2DN
Telephone: Godalming (0483) 861111

West Sussex County Council
County Hall, West Street, Chichester, West Sussex, PO19 1RL
Telephone: Chichester (0243) 777100

Buses: Since closure of the railway, a fairly complicated pattern of bus services has evolved. Those routes of use to the railway rambler are summarized in tables 1 and 2 below. The principal operators are as follows:

Alder Valley
Bus Station, The Friary, Guildford, Surrey
Telephone: Guildford (0483) 575226

Brighton & Hove Bus and Coach Company
43 Conway Street, Hove, East Sussex, BN3 3LT
Telephone: Brighton (0273) 206666

London Country South West
Lesbourne Road, Reigate, Surrey, RH2 7LE
Telephone: Reigate (0737) 242411

Southdown Motor Services Limited
Bus and Coach Station, Marine Parade, Worthing, West Sussex
Telephone: Worthing (0903) 37661

Trains: British Rail Telephone Enquiry Bureaux
Telephone: Brighton (0273) 206755
          or: Horsham (0403) 62218
          or: Woking (0483) 755905

A complicated pattern of bus services has developed since the lines closed. The service from Guildford to Horsham is the most convenient as it allows walkers to go as far as they wish and then return by bus. However, there is no through service from Horsham to Bramber so walks on this section require careful planning; tables 1 and 2 summarize the current services and destinations.

Table 1 – Bus Services in the vicinity of the Downs Link

Route	Service	Days	Frequency
Guildford–Cranleigh	AV 263	Mon–Sat	Hourly
Guildford–Cranleigh	AV 273	Daily	Hourly
Guildford–Horsham	AV 283	Mon–Sat	Hourly
Horsham–Christ's Hospital	LC H6	Mon–Sat	Four per day
Horsham–Southwater	LC H5	Mon–Sat	Hourly
Horsham–Brighton	SD 107	Mon–Sat	Hourly
Horsham–Brighton	SD 137	Mon–Sat	Two per day
Horsham–Brighton	AV not known	Sun	Three per day
Steyning–Brighton	BH 20, 20A, 20X	Daily	Hourly

AV: Alder Valley; BH: Brighton & Hove; LC: London Country; SD: Southdown.

Table 2 – Summary of Places served by Public Transport

Station/Former Station	Operator	Service
Guildford	British Rail	Frequent
Shalford (near Peasmarsh)	British Rail	Two-hourly, Mon–Sat
Bramley and Wonersh	Alder Valley	263, 273, 283
Cranleigh	Alder Valley	263, 273, 283
Rudgwick	Alder Valley	283
Slinfold	Alder Valley	283
Christ's Hospital	British Rail	Two-hourly, Mon–Sat
Christ's Hospital	London Country	H6
Southwater	London Country	H5
West Grinstead	Southdown	137
Partridge Green	Southdown	107
Henfield	Southdown	107
Steyning	Brighton & Hove	20, 20A, 20X
Bramber	Brighton & Hove	20, 20A, 20X
Shoreham	Brighton & Hove	20, 20A, 20X
Shoreham	British Rail	Up to four trains per hour

Readers are reminded that these services are liable to alteration and current details should be checked with the relevant operator.

There are plenty of pubs within easy reach of the Downs Link, the most convenient being the Thurlow Arms at Baynards, the Bridge House at Copsale and the Cat and Canary at Henfield; in all three cases, the walk passes within a few yards of the front door. For those with an interest in ale, the local brewer is King and Barnes of Horsham but the company has managed to site most of its pubs some distance from the walk; fortunately, its products are widely available in the free trade. On a practical note, walkers should remember that a few short sections of the Downs Link are rather boggy, even in good weather. Those who end up with a lot of mud on their boots might find it prudent to select a pub with a garden or public bar. This information is generally available in the CAMRA pub guides.

10
THE CUCKOO TRAIL
Polegate to Heathfield

Introduction

The South Downs Way runs from Eastbourne on the south coast to Buriton, a small Downland village a few miles from Petersfield in Hampshire. Many walkers get to the start of the route by taking the train to Eastbourne, and those who travel from London or Brighton may notice the small wayside station of Polegate, two stops before their destination. Nowadays the station is a most unprepossessing affair; the bland modern building opened in summer 1988 does not have much in the way of architectural merit.

It is therefore rather surprising to discover that Polegate was once a substantial railway junction with extensive sidings and lines radiating out in four separate directions, to Eridge in the north, Hastings in the east, Eastbourne in the south and Brighton in the west. It is also surprising to discover that the station has had a rather peripatetic existence. The present building is the third Polegate station and marks a return to the original site which was abandoned in 1881. Being just off the High Street, this is certainly more convenient for intending passengers but then the nineteenth-century railway was never averse to demanding a long walk if operating convenience so demanded.

The line from Polegate to Eridge was named 'The Cuckoo Line' by the railwaymen themselves. This derives from a Sussex tradition that the first cuckoo of spring is released each year at Heathfield Fair by an old woman who keeps them all throughout the winter months. The fair is held annually on 14 April, but visitors beware: she only comes if she is in a good mood!

History

The first railway line to reach Polegate was that from Brighton to Bulverhythe, west of Hastings. The section from Brighton to Lewes was laid as double track

As the result of a deep cutting, the station buildings at Heathfield were on a different level to the track. The station was some little way from the town of the same name

Lens of Sutton

and opened on 8 June 1846, the single-track extension to Bulverhythe following a few weeks later on 27 June. This arrangement lasted barely three years, Polegate becoming a four-way junction on 14 May 1849 with the simultaneous opening of lines to both Hailsham and Eastbourne. It is interesting to note that, earlier in the century, Eastbourne had been nothing more than a huddle of buildings around the church and the Lamb Inn but, by this date, was beginning to eclipse the market town of Hailsham in size and importance.

Hailsham was to remain the northern terminus of the branch for thirty-one years, a fact still witnessed by the Terminus Hotel which stands nearby. This arrangement resulted in a very circuitous route to London and other more local destinations, in consequence of which local businessmen promoted a bill in 1873 for a 3 ft narrow gauge line which would link Polegate and Tunbridge Wells. The South Eastern Railway became interested and developed the scheme into a proposed standard gauge line between Eastbourne and Tunbridge Wells, but there were difficulties in raising the necessary capital. Things remained uncertain until 1876, when the London, Brighton and South Coast Railway obtained an Act of Parliament which effectively allowed it to take over the existing scheme and thus provide the new route by extending its own line beyond Hailsham. The extension from Hailsham to Heathfield was accordingly opened on 5 April 1880, with the section from Heathfield to Eridge following on 1 September of the same year. Residents of Hailsham and Eastbourne now had direct access both to Tunbridge Wells via Groombridge and London via Oxted.

At Polegate, the junctions for Eastbourne and the Cuckoo Line both faced west. This was fine for trains originating at Brighton but forced new services from Eastbourne to Tunbridge Wells to reverse at Polegate. In order to eliminate this, substantial alterations were carried out at Polegate between 1880 and 1881: the junction with the Cuckoo Line was altered to face Eastbourne and a grand new station constructed a quarter of a mile east of the original. The main part of this still stands alongside Station Road and now serves as a pub/restaurant, but the four platforms have been razed to the ground. The station acquired a very forlorn appearance during the 1970s due to lack of maintenance and the removal of the canopies, so this renovation is probably just as well.

After 1881 Polegate station settled down to a long, and generally uneventful, working life. The most notorious event in its history occurred on 12 January 1920, when a group of platelayers boarded a Hastings-bound train and discovered the battered victim of an unknown assailant. Miss Florence Nightingale Shore, a nurse, was still conscious but unable to speak or to move and died of her injuries four days later in East Sussex Hospital, Bexhill. No shred of evidence or information connected with this crime has ever come to light.

The Cuckoo Line ran mainly through attractive hilly countryside (particularly north of Horam) and, being cheaply constructed, featured many steep gradients and sharp curves. In its early days, the crews of late-running trains were tempted to make up time by speeding down gradients but, in 1897, a driver was killed when he apparently tried this expedient and derailed his train north of Heathfield, causing several passengers to be injured in the process. The poor quality of the track and the tight schedules of the timetable were singled out for blame, but the accident also resulted in a special warning against 'running down inclines' in subsequent working timetables.

The first station on the line was at Hailsham. This was its terminus from 1849 to 1880 and reverted to that status again from 1965 to 1968. Hellingly was next and this remained the only station on the branch without a passing loop. It enjoyed a quiet existence serving the needs of a scattered rural community until 1899, when work began on constructing the massive 'East Sussex Asylum', later Hellingly Mental Hospital. The contractors installed a standard gauge branch, which ran from Hellingly station to the hospital and was used initially to convey their building materials. When the hospital was completed in 1903, the county council purchased the contractors' railway and, remarkably in this out-of-the-way spot, electrified it using 500 Volts DC and an early overhead catenary system. A timber platform was provided at Hellingly for hospital branch passengers but

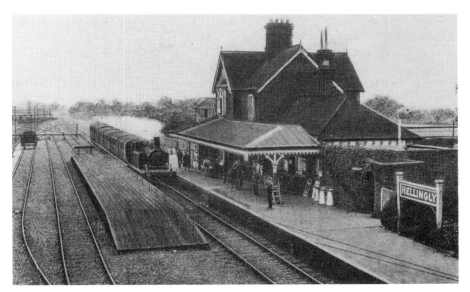

Hellingly station on the line from Polegate to Eridge. Alongside the 'main' line here was a short branch serving the nearby hospital, which was one of the first to use the overhead electric wire system. The catenary masts on the left are in stark conrtrast to the steam train at the main station

Lens of Sutton

this traffic ceased in 1931 and the platform was removed in 1932. However, freight traffic continued until March 1959 by which time it was a modest two wagons of coal per day. This was used for the hospital's boilers and generators which, of course, also provided power for the 14 hp electric locomotive; an apparent case of self-perpetuation. The line was closed when the hospital switched to oil, a final enthusiasts' special running on 4 March 1959.

Horam station was the third up the branch. It was so called in 1935, previous incarnations being Horeham Road for Waldron, Horeham Road and Waldron, and Waldron and Horeham Road. These variations suggest that, originally, the station served nowhere in particular but, for all that, it was an attractive building with a half-timbered finish and embossed patterns in the plasterwork. Unfortunately, the plaster allowed water penetration over the years, as a result of which the architect's fine decorative touches had to be covered with hung tiles. This would have been a less than perfect solution if the nails rusted, but the whole site was flattened before this could become a problem. In 1988, the area had a desolate appearance and awaited redevelopment.

Heathfield came next. This was an important station for freight and had the distinction of being the starting point for a small number of trains which did not travel the whole length of the line. Heathfield was also unique in having its own supply of natural gas. This was reported originally in a survey of 1875 and confirmed twenty years later in the course of drilling a well for the Heathfield Hotel. However, no water was found and so the bore was sealed. The following year (1896), the LBSCR sank its own borehole, apparently unaware of the hotel's earlier failure, and at 312 ft encountered a considerable stench and 'rushing of wind'. Someone lit a match to investigate and the resulting flame, some 16 ft tall, proved beyond all doubt that the railway had discovered natural gas. It is hardly surprising that the workmen had some difficulty in putting the flame out!

This supply lit the station from 1898 until 1934, by which time for all practical purposes it was exhausted. However, the gas continued to be received by two gas-holders which stood to the north-east of the station, just beyond the existing road bridge. From these, it was compressed into cylinders and conveyed by rail to a laboratory which tested flameproof electric motors for use in mines. The bore was finally sealed in 1963 when the gas supply had dwindled still further.

The seasoned railway rambler is well used to walking old lines which had sparse services. Not so the Cuckoo Line. In 1961/2, it enjoyed twenty-four north-bound and twenty-five south-bound trains per day. Admittedly, a few terminated at Hailsham or Heathfield but, set against this, the 7.58 a.m. from Eastbourne travelled over the line and conveyed through carriages for Victoria; these arrived at 10.21 a.m. and formed a return working at 10.38. This is hardly the picture of a railway in decline and, until the publication of the Beeching Report in 1963, the Southern Region was still trying to encourage traffic.

Dr Beeching's arrival changed things dramatically. In *Forgotten Railways of South East England*, H.P. White suggests that the Southern Region may have been forced to contribute its share of line closures. If this is true, it is understandable that it should sacrifice steam and diesel lines rather than modernized electric routes. Unfortunately, a large proportion of the doomed lines ran through the Weald of Sussex.

The real damage began to be inflicted in 1964 when the passenger timetable was recast. This was partly to reflect changes in travel patterns but at the same time, disturbingly, the tightly woven network of inter-connecting services on many routes was broken. Passengers who for years had enjoyed short and convenient connections now found themselves confronted with long delays, allegedly designed to deter them from using services on lines that had been proposed for closure. If this was the case, it is much to their credit that, according to a 1965 survey, an average 250 passengers per day were still using Cuckoo Line services.

But the closure notices had already been posted. Passenger services north of Hailsham were withdrawn on 14 June 1965. Freight services to Heathfield survived until 26 April 1968 but then a bridge was damaged and repair considered uneconomical; the line was abandoned instead. Modern diesel trains continued to ply between Eastbourne and Hailsham until 9 September 1968, but then they too disappeared into the history books.

The Line Today

The northern section from Heathfield to Eridge was the first to close entirely and its disposal was rather piecemeal. Today, the local authority owns a few short stretches but, for the most part, the old railway is in private hands and there is no public access. However, the story south of Heathfield is rather different. British Rail retained the trackbed to Polegate until 1981, when it was purchased by East Sussex County and Wealden District councils. The county was concerned with the urban stretch within Hailsham (which it thought might be used for road improvements), while the district took over the rest. Happily, the county highways committee has now declared the Hailsham trackbed surplus to requirements, thus allowing its designation as a walkway.

The whole of the line has enjoyed this status for some years but, in the early days, a lack of commitment or resources resulted in a low level of maintenance. Several commentators have remarked upon this and, indeed, no rambler who has ever struggled through the muddy morass north of Polegate could miss it. However, in January 1988, Wealden District Council formed a working party to develop proposals for the route's improvement and these were approved in full in October that year. As a result, walkers on the Cuckoo Trail can expect to find an amenity which, like the best wine, improves as the years go by.

The Walk (10 miles)

It is easiest to tackle this walk from south to north. This allows for arrival by train and avoids the problem of walking into the sun – if it should happen to shine!

Starting from Polegate station, the walker should proceed to the High Street (by the level crossing) and there turn right. This leads past the Dinkum (a public house named by ANZACs who used it during the war) to a T-junction with Station Road; the Heathfield buses stop here outside the nearby Horse and Groom. The walker should then turn right again and first left in about 200 yds; the start of the railway path will be found on the right at grid reference 584052.

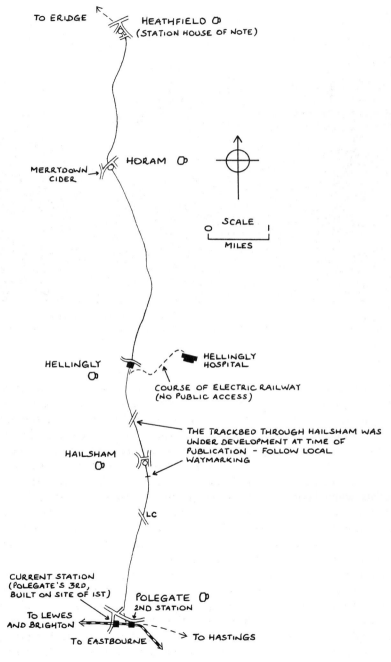

TO ERIDGE
HEATHFIELD ⊙
(STATION HOUSE OF NOTE)

MERRYDOWN
CIDER
HORAM ⊙

SCALE
MILES

HELLINGLY
⊙
HELLINGLY
HOSPITAL

COURSE OF ELECTRIC RAILWAY
(NO PUBLIC ACCESS)

THE TRACKBED THROUGH HAILSHAM WAS
UNDER DEVELOPMENT AT TIME OF
PUBLICATION – FOLLOW LOCAL
WAYMARKING

HAILSHAM
⊙

LC

CURRENT STATION
(POLEGATE'S 3RD,
BUILT ON SITE OF 1ST)

POLEGATE ⊙
2ND STATION

TO LEWES
AND BRIGHTON

TO EASTBOURNE
TO HASTINGS

The Cuckoo Trail

Crossing keeper's cottage between Polegate and Hailsham, much altered since the railway left. Soon the only clue as to its origin will be its alignment with the nearby Cuckoo Trail

The path begins in a wooded cutting but this is soon left behind as the line moves into open country with hills to the west and levels to the east. It then passes two minor roads, where the odd gate post still betrays the site of a level crossing. Beyond the second of these (grid reference 585060), the going is exceptionally muddy and wellington boots will remain essential until the district council's five-year work programme is complete. Horses were the immediate cause of the damage but the Water Authority may also have removed base materials when laying a new sewerage pipe to Hailsham North Works – a formidable combination. The resultant quagmire means that the walker must be very careful where he puts his feet; this makes it difficult to appreciate the surrounding countryside, but at least the council is aware of the problem and has budgetted a large sum for its correction.

The site of another level crossing follows at grid reference 588077, where the keeper's cottage still provides a link with the past. It is then an uneventful walk into Hailsham, where a new housing estate occupies the substantial railway yard that once existed to the south of the station. Nothing remains of the attractive Tudor-style station building, but the station-master's house still stands and, to the north of the site, there is an old bridge which carries the A295 over the now empty trackbed. This is underpinned with substantial timbers and is obviously

Bridge between Hellingly and Horam – easily wide enough for double track, though this was never laid

long past its prime, but it still bears traces of Southern Region paint and shelters a small fragment of the northbound platform ramp. Until 1988, the site suffered the ignominy of being used as a lorry park.

The next section of the trail belongs to East Sussex County Council and, when I visited, awaited improvement. It consists of a cutting half a mile long, followed by another housing estate where contractors have obliterated the route. To compound matters, the cutting had been used for dumping, with the result that it had flooded and was quite unsuitable for recreational walking. The importance of this apparently unpromising urban stretch is that it provides a valuable direct link between the north and south rural sections; it is to be hoped that the district council will be successful in persuading its 'big brother' to help develop the railway path as an amenity.

The line can be regained at grid reference 585105 (the site of a former overbridge) and it is then just over a mile to Hellingly station. After the rather depressing scene at Hailsham, this is a welcome relief. The station building survives intact, complete with integral canopy, and is now used as a private residence. The walker should take time to admire the fine decorative motifs in the plasterwork and note also the size of the now empty yard where electric trains from the hospital branch once ran.

In the next four miles to Horam, the line begins to climb and assumes a more wooded character. There are several attractive overbridges on this section and, south of Horam, the council has already completed some very welcome works to improve drainage and stabilize the surface. The site of Horam station is met at grid reference 578174 but, although it survived closure by several years, the station building remained unused, fell into disrepair and was demolished. The platforms were still intact in 1988, complete with empty station nameboards and a few concrete lamp-posts, but the site was due for redevelopment. Although the railway path is allowed for in the plans, it is highly unlikely that any trace of the station will survive.

The final two and a half miles to Heathfield feature rather more earthworks than previously. A high embankment leads out of Horam and there are some excellent views to the west across Waldron Gill. This is real 'Garden of England' country and, from his high viewpoint, the rambler looks down on the crowns of trees, lush green meadows and grazing sheep. On a more prosaic note, a number of new concrete bridges reveal the council's commitment to the path; only traffic noise from the nearby B2203 mars the effect.

New residential properties are met to the south of Heathfield. Some owners have purchased the edges of the old trackbed and extended their gardens onto it, but at least a clear route through has been preserved. It is also reassuring to discover that the council has stopped this practice following the recommendations of its 1988 working party.

The trail ends at grid reference 581213 where the passenger buildings of Heathfield station once stood. This was a grand affair, built on a site excavated out of a hillside, and offered the Victorian railway traveller every convenience: an elaborate covered footbridge connected the two platforms, which each boasted a substantial wooden building and long canopy. Today, a small industrial estate stands in the path of any would-be ghost trains; nothing of railway significance remains except the south portal of Heathfield Tunnel, to which there is no public access. However, the brick-built station house and main entrance survive in the street above and are used as a private residence.

Overall, the course of the old Cuckoo Line has had a very lucky escape. The review carried out by Wealden District Council in 1988 came at just the right time and brought to an end policies which would have had a very damaging effect on its recreational use. As a result, the sale of marginal land has been stopped and horse-riding suspended on severely damaged sections until improvements to the surface are complete; these will need to be extremely good to prevent any recurrence of the problem. Mercifully, the cuttings along the line were deemed too small and difficult of access to provide economic sites for waste disposal.

The future looks much brighter. While the council does not have a bottomless pocket, it has budgetted realistic sums for route improvements and these concentrate on those tasks which will turn the trail into an all-weather, all-year-round amenity; this alone will guarantee it a good level of use and thereby justify the investment. The provision of a ranger service is seen as a long-term possibility but, above all, there seems to be a genuine commitment to develop the facility. Many railway paths in the south of England have been developed with cut-price and half-hearted policies which result in their being sub-standard and under-utilized amenities. Wealden District Council has an excellent opportunity here to show others how it should be done.

Further Explorations

North of Heathfield, most Cuckoo Line trains called at Mayfield, Rotherfield and Mark Cross, Eridge, Groombridge and Tunbridge Wells West. The stations remain but only at Eridge is it still possible to catch a train. Mayfield is a particularly attractive village much loved by photographers from country magazines; the station was conveniently situated at its west end. Patrons of the next station were not so lucky, as its name suggests, but it was a longer walk to Mark Cross than Rotherfield. At Eridge, passengers could change onto connecting services for Brighton via Lewes or London via Oxted.

Eridge still enjoys an hourly service to London but trains to Brighton ceased on 23 February 1969 when British Rail closed the section from Uckfield to Lewes. The county council has protected most of the trackbed from development with a view to possible reinstatement and the Milham family has made a fine job of restoring the intermediate station at Isfield, which is now the headquarters of their Lavender Line. It was an overgrown wilderness when they acquired it on 16 June 1983 at an auction in Isfield village hall – an act of some impulsiveness and inspiration!

The last train from Eridge to Tunbridge Wells ran on 6 July 1985, although empty rolling stock continued to be stabled at Tunbridge Wells West for a few months after. The trains were not well used but, by the end, the line had shrunk to a purely local significance, closure of the Uckfield–Lewes section having destroyed all through traffic for Brighton and the Sussex coast. A preservation society has been formed which hopes to restore services by tapping into the lucrative Tunbridge Wells tourist trade and, if the line south of Uckfield is relaid as well, trains might once again ply between Tunbridge Wells and Brighton. All this is highly speculative, of course, but whatever the future holds, the fine Victorian station at Tunbridge Wells West should survive as it is now a listed building.

After Eridge, Groombridge offered Cuckoo Line passengers their next travel opportunities: a change of train here gave access to East Grinstead, where a further change could be made for Three Bridges near the new town of Crawley.

Both of these lines have been converted into local authority walks and both pass through delightful countryside. The line from Groombridge to East Grinstead has been designated the Forest Way and is managed by East Sussex, while that from East Grinstead to Three Bridges has been designated the Worth Way and is managed by West Sussex. Further details can be obtained from the respective county headquarters at Lewes and Chichester.

Further to the east, enthusiasts can sample the delights of the Kent and East Sussex Railway based at Tenterden in Kent. This commemorates the career of Còl. Holman Frederick Stephens who, in his time, collected ramshackle country branch lines in the way that a modern collector might amass vintage cars. The rolling stock on some of these lines was extraordinary, to say the least, and included a number of early Ford and Sheflex railcars of rather comical appearance. The colonel was enterprising, if nothing else, but some of his lines were in such a poor financial state that he had to buy vehicles like this himself. The official receiver was called in to the Kent and Sussex in 1932 but, miraculously, it struggled on until 1948 when it was taken over by the newly-created British Railways. The new owners were less forbearing than the receiver and closed the line to passengers in 1954, although the occasional pick-up goods and hop-pickers' special ran as late as July 1961. The modern Kent and East Sussex Railway re-opened the line from Tenterden to Rolvenden in February 1974 and is extending steadily westwards. Like the Isle of Wight Steam Railway, this is a preservation scheme with a distinctly different flavour.

Transport and Facilities

Map: Ordnance Survey: Landranger Series Sheet 199 (recommended)

Buses: Southdown Motor Services Limited
32 Cavendish Place, Eastbourne, East Sussex, BN21 3HY
Telephone : Eastbourne (0323) 27354

Trains: British Rail Telephone Enquiry Bureaux
Telephone: Brighton (0273) 206755
    or: Hastings (0452) 429325

Heathfield is one of the major towns in the Weald and this no doubt accounts for it still having a reasonable bus service. Even more remarkably, a significant proportion of its bus passengers travel to Hailsham and Eastbourne with the happy result that Southdown operates a regular service which still calls at the same towns and villages as the former railway. This is service 728, which runs hourly from Heathfield (High Street) to Polegate (Horse and Groom) on the A27, the last bus leaving Heathfield at approximately 7.00 p.m. Experienced ramblers will appreciate that this is a very fortunate state of affairs, for many bus services now bisect old lines rather than run parallel to them.

A glance at the map will show that the Cuckoo Trail marches across some fairly quiet rural backwaters, but there is no problem in finding pubs or other facilities near the various station sites. Those with a taste for local ales may like to keep an eye out for Harveys of Lewes but, regrettably, this small family brewer is not widely represented in the area. Perhaps thirsty walkers would consider some local cider instead?

Cider, by all accounts, originated as a south-eastern drink and was widely made in Sussex and Kent before migrating to the West Country where its fame (or infamy!) now chiefly resides. In recent years, various concerns have tried to revive the tradition in the south-east, none more successfully than Merrydown who are based at Horam Manor, a short walk from the old Horam station. While their traditional draught cider is not widely available, their bottled ciders are easily found and can be recommended for their clean taste and refreshing champagne style.

APPENDIX A

Useful Addresses

RAILWAY RAMBLERS
Membership Secretary,
47a Stondon Park,
Forest Hill,
London,
SE23 7LB

DAVID ARCHER
Secondhand Maps,
The Pentre,
Kerry,
Newtown,
Powys,
Wales,
SY16 4PD

THE BRANCH LINE SOCIETY
73 Norfolk Park Avenue,
Sheffield,
South Yorkshire,
S2 2RB

CAMRA LTD
The Campaign for Real Ale,
34 Alma Road,
St Albans,
Hertfordshire,
AL1 3BW

CHEDDAR VALLEY RAILWAY
WALK SOCIETY
Membership Secretary,
Mrs B. Jevons,
Lanacre,
Sidcot Lane,
Winscombe, Avon

DEVON COUNTY COUNCIL
Amenities and Countryside
Division,
Property Department,
County Hall,
Exeter, Devon

RAMBLERS' ASSOCIATION
1/5 Wandsworth Road,
London,
SW8 2XX

SUSTRANS LTD/RAILWAY
PATH PROJECT
35 King Street,
Bristol,
BS1 4DZ

WEY AND ARUN CANAL
TRUST LTD
24 Griffiths Avenue,
Lancing, West Sussex

Note: CAMRA's local pub guides contain much valuable information for walkers and are thoroughly recommended. The majority of them show which pubs offer food, when they are open, whether they have gardens and whether they have public bars.

APPENDIX B

Official Railway Walks

Very few railway paths are dedicated public rights of way. The majority are 'permissive routes'; that is, the landowner (usually a county council or other public body) permits their use by pedestrians and, occasionally, horseriders and/or cyclists. As such, they may *very occasionally* be closed, e.g. to permit repairs to the surface.

This list deals only with the major routes in each county, although it should be noted that in some counties two miles would be a long railway walk. As a result, the list has been tailored to reflect the longest of what is available. It should also be noted that some of the start points are not easily found: if in difficulty, enquire locally or obtain a copy of the excellent *Railway Rights of Way* by Rhys ab Elis. This encyclopaedia of railway walk information is published by the Branch Line Society and is remarkably good value at around £4, including supplements. It gives a comprehensive list of railway walks, however small, throughout the British Isles and, on a practical level, provides grid references for most of the start and end points.

The following codes indicate the suitability of each walk for wheelchair users:

A Usable throughout
B Usable in places
C Generally unusable
X Route not inspected

It is a good idea to contact the relevant authority (i.e. county council, district council, Sustrans or whoever) before using these walks as there are a number of practical difficulties. Even a walk which can accommodate a wheelchair throughout may have access controlled by locked gates. Such devices are intended to keep out motor cycles but, unfortunately, they also restrict legitimate and deserving users; your assistant may therefore need to obtain a key. If this is the case, please ensure that all gates are locked securely behind you. The best bet will always be a path constructed by Sustrans Ltd or built according to its principles. A glance at the following list reveals that most other routes need upgrading before the disabled can use them with anything approaching ease and comfort.

If your immediate area does not have any suitable facilities, it will do no harm to draw their absence to the attention of the local authority. Surprising as it may seem, a number of English counties have converted no abandoned trackbeds into 'rail trails' at all, while others have provided a service which is not consistently wide or smooth enough for wheelchair use. Councils are unlikely to make improvements if they are not informed of the demand for, and the benefits of, this type of reclamation work. Some of the arguments in favour of railway paths and cycleways are set out in the Introduction; they may prove helpful in drafting a letter.

Avon

Yatton–Axbridge (8 miles) *C*
Bath–Bristol (15 miles) *A*
Radstock–Midsomer Norton (2 miles) *C*

Berkshire

No railway walks.

Cornwall

Truro–Newham (1½ miles) *C*
The Camel Trail, comprising:
    a. Padstow–Wadebridge–Bodmin (12½ miles) *A*
    b. Boscarne Junction–Wenfordbridge (6 miles) *B*

Devon

Plymouth (Marsh Mills)–Goodameavy (6 miles) *A*
Barnstaple–Bideford (6½ miles) *A*
Barnstaple–Braunton (5½ miles) *C*
Ilfracombe–Mortehoe (3 miles) *X*
Dousland–Princetown (8 miles) *C*
Bittaford–Red Lake (Red Lake Tramway) (9 miles) *C*

Part of the Haytor Granite Tramway is also being included in a new route known as The Templer Way; when complete, this will run from Haytor to Newton Abbot connecting with a riverside path to Shaldon. A walkers leaflet is available from the Amenities and Countryside Division of Devon County Council.

Dorset

Wimborne (Oakley)–Upton (4 miles) *A*

The Dorset Naturalists Trust has also taken over part of the delightful Bridport branch in the vicinity of Witherstone bank, the notorious incline north-east of Powerstock.

Gloucestershire

Stonehouse–Nailsworth (5½ miles) *A*
Withington–Chedworth (3 miles) *X*
South Cerney–Cricklade (3½ miles) *X*
The Forest of Dean railway paths, comprising:
    a. Parkend–Drybrook Road (4½ miles) *B*
    b. Moseley Green–Drybrook Road (4½ miles) *C*
    c. Mierystock–Drybrook Road (2½ miles) *C*

Hampshire

Knowle Junction–West Meon (11 miles) *B*
Mottisfont (Stonymarsh)–Fullerton Junction (9 miles) *C*
Ringwood–Ashley Heath (2 miles) *X*
Havant–Hayling Island (5 miles)★ *A*
Brockenhurst (Cater's Cottage)–Burbush Hill (7 miles) *B*
Gosport–Stokes Bay (2 miles)★ *B*
Gosport–Fort Brockhurst (3 miles) *B*
Litchfield–Burghclere (3 miles) *C*

★ At the time of publication a few breaks in the continuity of these routes were still present.

Isle of Wight

Cowes–Newport (4½ miles) *A*
Shanklin–Wroxall (2½ miles) *C*
Yarmouth–Freshwater (2½ miles) *B*
Horringford–Sandown (3 miles) *C*

Kent

No railway walks.

London

Only very minor lengths of trackbed have been preserved in Greater London.

Oxfordshire

No railway walks.

Somerset

Brushford (near Dulverton)–Nightcott (1½ miles) *C*

Watchet–Washford (2 miles on course of former mineral railway) *X*
Axbridge–Cheddar (1¼ miles)⋆ *A*

⋆ See also entry under Avon for Yatton–Axbridge, with which this route connects.

Surrey

Only very minor lengths of trackbed have been preserved in the county, but see entry under West Sussex for the Downs Link which starts in Surrey.

Sussex, East

East Grinstead–Groombridge (9 miles) *B*
Polegate–Heathfield (10 miles) *B*

Sussex, West

Three Bridges–East Grinstead (6 miles) *C*
The Downs Link, comprising:
   a. Peasmarsh–Christ's Hospital (15½ miles) *B*
   b. Christ's Hospital–Bramber (14½ miles) *B*

Wiltshire

Chiseldon–Marlborough (7½ miles) *A*
Swindon Old Town–Rushey Platt (1½ miles) *A*

APPENDIX C

County Council Public Transport Offices

Following deregulation of the buses in October 1986, it is now more difficult than ever to obtain information about rural bus services. The following county council public transport offices will help walkers overcome this problem. Most of them are open normal office hours Mondays to Fridays (9 a.m.–5 p.m.) with a few opening extended hours including Saturdays.

Avon: Bristol (0272) 290777

Berkshire: Reading (0734) 581358

Cornwall: Truro (0872) 74282

Devon: Exeter (0392) 272123

Dorset: Dorchester (0305) 204537

Gloucestershire: Gloucester (0452) 425543

Hampshire: Winchester (0962) 841841

Isle of Wight: Isle of Wight (0983) 524031

Kent: Maidstone (0622) 671411

London: London (01) 222 1234

Oxfordshire: Oxford (0865) 810405

Somerset: Taunton (0823) 255696

Surrey: London (01) 541 9367

Sussex, East: Brighton (0273) 482123

Sussex, West: Chichester (0243) 777556

Wiltshire: Trowbridge (0225) 743641

BIBLIOGRAPHY

General

Appleton, Dr J.H., *Disused Railways in the Countryside of England and Wales*. HMSO, 1970.
Daniels, Gerald and Dench, Les, *Passengers No More*. Ian Allan, 1980.
Elis, Rhys ab, *Railway Rights of Way*. Branch Line Society, 1985.
Forgotten Railways, series by David and Charles.
John Grimshaw and Associates, *Study of Disused Railways in England and Wales* HMSO, 1982.
A Regional History of the Railways of Great Britain, series by David and Charles.

Atlases

Conolly, W. Philip, *British Railways Pre-Grouping Atlas and Gazetteer*. Ian Allan, 1972.
Wignall, C.J., *Complete British Railways Maps and Gazetteer*. Oxford Publishing Co., 1983.

Chapter 1

Hall, R.M.S., *The Lee Moor Tramway*. Oakwood Press, 1987.
Hemery, Eric, *Walking the Dartmoor Railroads*. David and Charles, 1983.
Mills, Bernard, *The Branch: Plymouth–Tavistock South–Launceston*. Plym Valley Railway Association, 1983.

Chapter 2

Cheddar Valley Railway Walk Society, *Cheddar Valley Railway Walk – A Proposal*. 1978.
Farr, Michael, Lovell, R., Maggs, Colin G., and Whetmath, Charles, *The Wrington Vale Light Railway*. Avon-Anglia Publications, 1978.
Hayes, R. and Shaw, M., *Railways in Wells*. HST/Wells Railway Fraternity, 1982.

Chapter 3

Paar, H.W., *The Severn & Wye Railway*. David and Charles, 1973
Pope, Ian, How, Bob and Karau, Paul, *The Severn & Wye Railway*. Wild Swan Publications, 1983.

Chapter 4

Nothing of any substance has been published on the Nailsworth branch.

Chapter 5

Barrett, David, Bridgeman, Brian and Bird, Denis, *A M & SWJR Album, Volume 1*: 1872–1899. Redbrick Publishing, 1981.
Maggs, Colin G., *The Midland & South Western Junction Railway*. David and Charles, 1967.
Sands, T.B., *The Midland & South Western Junction Railway*. The Oakwood Press, 1959.

Chapter 6

Fairclough, Tony and Wills, Alan, *Southern Branch Line Special No. 1, Bodmin and Wadebridge 1834–1978*. Bradford Barton, 1979.
Ingrey, Jack, *The Camel Footpath from Padstow to Wadebridge*. Lodenek Press, 1984.
Whetmath, C.F.D., *The Bodmin and Wadebridge Railway*. Town and Country Press, 1972.

Chapter 7

Cox, J.G., *Castleman's Corkscrew*. City of Southampton, 1975.
Popplewell, Lawrence, *Bournemouth Railway History*. Dorset Publishing Company, 1973.
Young, J.A., *The Ringwood, Christchurch and Bournemouth Railway*. Bournemouth Local Studies Publications, 1985.

Chapter 8

Hay, Peter, *Steaming Through the Isle of Wight*. Middleton Press, 1988.
Mitchell, Vic and Smith, Keith, *Branch Lines to Newport*. Middleton Press, 1985.
Mitchell, Vic and Smith, Keith, *South Coast Railways – Ryde to Ventnor*. Middleton Press, 1985.

Chapter 9

Course, Edwin, *The Railways of Southern England: Secondary and Branch Lines*. Batsford, 1974.
Mitchell, Vic and Smith, Keith, *Branch Lines to Horsham*. Middleton Press, 1982.
Oppitz, Leslie, *Sussex Railways Remembered*. Countryside Books, 1987.

Chapter 10

Hay, Peter, *Steaming Through East Sussex*. Middleton Press, 1985.
Mitchell, Vic and Smith, Keith, *Branch Lines to Tunbridge Wells*. Middleton Press, 1986.
Oppitz, Leslie, *Sussex Railways Remembered*. Countryside Books, 1987.
Roberts, Mick, 'Suddenly it's the Lavender Line', *Steam Railway*, No. 56, December 1984.

INDEX

Wallbridge, 60, 62
Wells, 15, 16, 17, 18, 26, 28
Wenfordbridge, 78, 80, 83, 86, 88, 89, 153
West Grinstead, 121, 126, 132
Weston-super-Mare, 15, 18, 28, 53
Wildlife, 10, 20, 24, 42, 85, 99, 113, 132
Wimberry, 32, 33
Wimborne, 91, 92, 93, 97, 98, 101, 154

Winscombe, 16, 19, 23, 28
Witham, 15, 16, 18, 19
Woodborough, *see* Winscombe
Woodchester, 54, 55, 56, 63
Wookey, 16, 27
Wroxall, 112, 114, 154

Yarmouth, 114, 115, 154
Yatton, 15–20 *passim*, 22, 24, 25, 26, 28, 153
Yelverton, 2, 4, 13, 14